The Deathly Embrace

Orientalism and Asian American Identity

Sheng-mei Ma

University of Minnesota Press

Minneapolis

London

Portions of chapter 5 originally appeared in *The Lion and the Unicorn* 23.2 (April 1999): 202–18. Chapter 8 originally appeared in *Post Identity* 2.1 (Spring 1999): 52–69.

Published by the University of Minnesota Press
111 Third Avenue South, Suite 290
Minneapolis, MN 55401-2520
http://www.upress.umn.edu

Library of Congress Cataloging-in-Publication Data

Ma, Sheng-mei.
    The deathly embrace : orientalism and Asian American identity / Sheng-mei Ma.
        p.   cm.
    Includes bibliographical references (p.   ) and index.
    ISBN 0-8166-3710-5 (alk. paper) — ISBN 0-8166-3711-3 (pbk. : alk. paper)
        1. Asian Americans — Ethnic identity.   2. Asian Americans — Cultural assimilation.   3. Orientalism — United States.   4. Asian Americans and mass media.   5. American literature — Asian American authors — History and criticism.   I. Title.
    E184.O6 M22 2000
    305.895073 — dc21   00-008866

Printed in the United States of America on acid-free paper

The University of Minnesota is an equal-opportunity educator and employer.

11 10 09 08 07 06 05 04 03 02 01 00   10 9 8 7 6 5 4 3 2 1

For Yaya
who has taught me about childhood and,
well, Disney

Contents

Acknowledgments

I completed this manuscript under the auspices of the Rockefeller Foundation Fellowship, 1997–98, jointly administered by Tani Barlow and Ann Anagnost at the University of Washington, where I was in residence that year. Tani and Ann's generous support through their Critical Asian Studies enabled me to bring this project to fruition. Leroy Searle, then director of the Center for the Humanities at the University of Washington, offered timely help to salvage my manuscript from a crashing computer hard drive. My publisher, the University of Minnesota Press, has handled my manuscript with tremendous professionalism. Douglas Armato, director of the Press, Gretchen Asmussen, executive assistant, and David Thorstad, copyeditor, have provided excellent suggestions for the manuscript and, in particular, the twenty-nine figures. The ideas contained herein are, needless to say, my sole responsibility.

At Michigan State University, a research leave granted by the College of Arts and Letters in fall 1996 allowed for a sustained period of time to reflect. It is my good fortune to have Douglas A. Noverr as my department chair, who has stood by me throughout the years. I am further blessed by the advice and friendship of Roger Jiang Bresnahan, my department mentor; Roger's generous personality contains this deep reserve for serving others.

For nearly three decades, from Taipei to Bloomington to Harrisonburg to Seattle and now to East Lansing, Lien has been the source of love and steadfastness, without which I would not have written this or any other thing.

Introduction

Contrary to the widely held assumption of their mutual exclusivity, Orientalism and Asian American identity were strange bedfellows in the 1970s, in the 1990s, and, I predict, will continue to be so in the twenty-first century. The struggle for ethnic identity presupposes a lack thereof, or a spurious identity imposed by Orientalism, the discursive tradition in the West dealing with the subject and the subjugation of the East. But in order to retire racist stereotypes, one is obliged to first evoke them; in order to construct ethnicity, one must first destruct what is falsely reported as one's ethnic identity. Both result in an unwitting reiteration of Orientalist images.

The term *Asian American,* inspired by the civil rights movement, was forged in the 1960s to empower heretofore disparate Asian American communities. Any construction of identity requires a reconfiguration, sometimes rather violently, of one's psyche and history. As a result, the groundbreaking texts in the formation of an Asian American literary tradition contain exactly such revolutionary, Yeatsian "terrible beauty." The two pivotal texts in the Asian American project, *Aiiieeeee! An Anthology of Asian American Writers* (1974) and Maxine Hong Kingston's *The Woman Warrior* (1976), are marked by the spirit of contestation in the attempt to wrest out of Orientalist grips an autonomous ethnic self. These two texts are joined, in the field of literary criticism, by Elaine Kim's equally pioneering *Asian American Literature* (1982). The preface to *Aiiieeeee!* and Kim's book try to establish a canon by attacking Western stereotypes of Asians, epitomized by Fu Manchu and Charlie Chan, by critiquing "inauthentic," Orientalist texts penned by immigrants and their descendants, and by valorizing "authentic" Asian American texts. These early attempts set a critical pattern for nearly all subsequent Asian American projects. Jessica Hagedorn even titles her anthology of contemporary Asian American writings *Charlie Chan Is Dead* (1993). Garrett Hongo displays similar conviction when he calls his anthology *Under Western Eyes: Personal Essays from Asian America* (1995). As for scholarly works focusing solely on "authentic" Asian American texts — for example, Sau-ling Cynthia Wong's *Reading Asian American Literature* (1993) and King-Kok Cheung's *Articulate Silences* (1993) — they presume that the reader is aware of the scourge of Orientalism, both in the Western mind and in those Asian American texts judged to have what the 1960s radicals called "false consciousness."

Orientalism and Asian American identity are thus ultimately symbiotic. Edward Said, whose *Orientalism* (1978) practically inaugurated postcolonial studies, espouses similar views in *Culture and Imperialism* (1993): "As we look at the cultural archive, we begin to reread it not univocally but *contrapuntally,* with a simultaneous awareness both of the metropolitan history that is narrated and of those other histories against which (and together with which) the dominating discourse acts" (51). The parenthesis suggests a possible symbiotic relationship between the metropolitan and the subaltern, since "We are, so to speak, *of* the connections, not outside or beyond them." For either one to pretend that the other has ceased to exist is a political posture.

Said's position in *Culture and Imperialism* is a revision from his previous one in *Orientalism,* which has been roundly criticized as a "totalizing" master narrative, ignoring counterhegemonic voices within the colonies as well as within the Western discourse. Said's critics invariably challenge his thesis of a monolithic Orientalism and, by implication, a hegemonic Occidentalism. Wrestling with Said are Dennis Porter from the critical angle of travel writings, John M. MacKenzie from historicism, Aijaz Ahmad from Marxism, and Lisa Lowe from the notion of heterogeneity, among others. That they are all compelled to rebut *Orientalism* testifies to the power of Said's book, which derives from a problematic intersection of Foucauldian discourse theory and Gramscian hegemony. Said defines Orientalism as

> a *distribution* of geopolitical awareness into aesthetic, scholarly, economic, sociological, historical, and philological texts; it is an *elaboration* not

only of a basic geographical distinction ... but also of a whole series of "interests". ... it not only creates but also maintains; it *is*, rather than expresses, a certain *will* or *intention* to understand, in some cases to control, manipulate, even to incorporate, what is a manifestly different (or alternative and novel) world. (12)

Inasmuch as one consciously avoids the pitfall of totalizing narrative, it stands to reason that some, surely not all, "Orientals" living in the West are interpellated by and internalize Orientalism, as there might be scarcely little in their American surroundings to counteract that dominant force of representation. The "distribution," the "elaboration," and the "will" to power are shared by minority subjects. Hence, Orientalist *mis*representations conceivably become *self*-representations.

As a result, the Orientalist formula applies in certain Asian American texts as well, where the Orient(al) is polarized, emptied of psychological depth and subjectivity. Echoing the extremes of Coleridge's "A sunny pleasure-dome with caves of ice!" in "Kubla Khan," the demonic and the domestic overlap in Asian America, with the exotic unfolding according to the most banal, overdetermined scheme. The West then projects its own neuroses onto the opposing constructs of, say, "Khans" and "Shangri-las," of the Mongolian horde and the Tibetan religiosity. In fact, only those Asian Americans who compose, more or less, in alignment with such Orientalism stand a chance in emerging among mainstream Western readers as representative ethnic voices. A prime example is Amy Tan. Pearl, Tan's protagonist in *The Kitchen God's Wife* (1991), for instance, adopts the white gaze at the moribund, otherworldly Chinatown in one of her reluctant homecoming visits:

As I turn down Ross Alley, everything around me immediately becomes muted in tone. It is no longer the glaring afternoon sun and noisy Chinatown sidewalks filled with people doing their Saturday grocery shopping. The alley sounds are softer, quickly absorbed, and the light is hazy, almost greenish in cast.

On the right-hand side of the street is the same old barbershop, run by Al Fook, who I notice still uses electric clippers to shear his customers' sideburns. Across the street are the same trade and family associations, including a place that will send ancestral memorials back to China for a fee. And farther down the street is the shopfront of a fortune-teller. A hand-written sign taped to the window claims to have "the best lucky numbers, the best fortune advice," but the sign taped to the door says: "Out of Business."

As I walk past the door, a yellow pull-shade rustles. And suddenly a
little girl appears, her hand pressed to the glass. She stares at me with a
somber expression. I wave, but she does not wave back. She looks at me
as if I don't belong here, which is how I feel. (18)

Chinatown, a Western invention embraced by the minority for survival,
is the closest a Chinese American can get to China. A dystopia in "muted"
tones, Chinatown betokens a dying culture, adorned with the 1950s sideburns and electric clippers, the Chinese tradition of ancestor worship,
and an out-of-business fortune-teller. In each of these three signifiers
of the community's demise, Pearl examines only the exteriority of the
construct in the attempt to confirm one's preconceptions of the Orient—that it is stagnant, hollow. As much an outsider to Chinatown as
any white tourist is bound to be, Pearl and Tan behind the scenes are
entirely unconcerned with the dynamics of business transaction, of kinship, and of the longing for prosperity within this ethnic community.
Even the minimal "voice" given to Chinatown proceeds in the ludicrous
pidgin of "the best lucky numbers, the best fortune advice." The final
paragraph further legitimizes white readers' distance by demonstrating
that even the protagonist, an erstwhile insider, has joined the majority.
Pearl used to be the little girl inside the glass window, but is now tour-
ing the site with the readers (indeed, Tan may be the best-paid tour guide
of Chinese America). What is on display is the somber, silent girl and
her ethnic community.

Prior to the civil rights movement, Asian American writers often
worked under, and many of them—like Tan at a later time—uncon-
sciously collaborated with, Western distortions of the East. This is readily apparent in the writings of Jade Snow Wong, Lin Yutang, and many
others. But even the distinguished careers of post-1960s Asian American
writers such as Kingston, Tan, Frank Chin, and David Henry Hwang
reveal that while the Asian American identity is constructed in reaction
to Orientalism, the two cultural forces are not necessarily at odds. By
contrast, Nisei writers such as Toshio Mori, Hisaye Yamamoto, and Joy
Kogawa, in their understated and self-restrained style, seldom dwell on
a phantasmagoric Orient or the bewildering Oriental. Although treasured by ethnic scholars, they are lesser known to the larger society and
belong perhaps to a different book. It is the collective writings of Kingston and her company that have created the image of Asian Americans
for the West. And with respect to these eminent representatives of Asian

America, Orientalism, to some extent, sires ethnicity, the former being the illegitimate patriarch disowned by the offspring. The vigor with which these Asian Americans revolt against Orientalism tacitly acknowledges the family lineage of the two. That Asian America is more than 150 years old but rebels like a misguided fifteen-year-old attests to its stunted growth, having been orphaned by the parent countries and then abused by the (step)parent of the United States.

An adult, nonetheless, revisits in good time that which he or she took leave of. Therefore, to review the multitude of historical forms appropriated by the deathly embrace of Orientalism and Asian American identity, this book highlights four types of cultural encounters, embodied in four metaphors of physical postures/states: *clutch of rape* in imperialist adventure narratives of the 1930s and 1940s; *clash of arms* or martial metaphors of the 1970s and beyond; U.S. multicultural *flaunting* of ethnicity; and global postcolonial *masquerading* of ethnicity. These four moments are not sharply segmented; rather, they overlap and intervene into one another.

It appears outrageous to implicate the editors of *Aiiieeeee!* and the author of *The Woman Warrior* in Orientalizing, for these artists have led the crusade of "claiming America" for Asian Americans for decades. The preface to the 1974 *Aiiieeeee!*, for example, opens with the urgent call for Asian American voices in order to smash the stereotype of an Oriental shrieking the incomprehensible "Aiiieeeee!"

> Our anthology is exclusively Asian American. That means Filipino, Chinese, and Japanese Americans, American born and raised, who got their China and Japan from the radio, off the silver screen, from television, out of comic books, from the pushers of white American culture that pictured the yellow man as something that when wounded, sad, or angry, or swearing, or wondering whined, shouted, or screamed "aiiieeeee!" Asian America, so long ignored and forcibly excluded from creative participation in American culture, is wounded, sad, angry, swearing, and wondering, and this is his AIIIEEEEE!!! It is more than a whine, shout, or scream. It is fifty years of our whole voice. (xi–xii)[1]

"American born and raised" points to the cultural nationalism of the early 1970s when American nativity was the prerequisite for Asian American identity. Accordingly, the editors maintain that Asian Americans "have evolved cultures and sensibilities distinctly not Chinese or Japanese and distinctly not white American" (xi). But this alleged autonomous identity is being proclaimed in a language so tortuous that it suggests a deep involvement with the majority culture. Note, in the preceding citation, the repetition of the second and the third sentences, the former renouncing the Orientalist image fabricated by the hegemony, the latter asserting Asian American ethnicity on the basis of that image. The third sentence uncannily locates the genesis of ethnicity in the linguistic distortion of "Aiiieeeee." This exclamation seems to be a reductive stylization of the Chinese sigh or cry "Aiya." Should this conjecture be accurate, the editors then fail to forge a unique existence by coining a new expression. Instead, they truncate the Chinese "Aiya" and suffix it with the long "e" sound from the racist pidgin in hope of turning a source of shame and oppression into a source of pride and emancipation. Of course, it is a common practice for minority groups to reinvent themselves by transforming preexisting stereotypes and by manipulating the master's language. African American youths, for instance, sometimes refer to one another as "niggers." In a different context, the Star of David, once used by the Nazis to signal vermin to be exterminated, adorns the national flag of Israel. Even with the long history of the Star of David as a Jewish symbol, one that predates Nazism, the memory of the Holocaust is deliberately evoked in the Israeli choice. Nonetheless, both the African American and the Israeli remakes of symbols of suffering highlight the problematics of refuting and acceding to hegemonic domination. In the case of *Aiiieeeee!*, the editors have unwittingly turned Asian American voices into both heckles against and echoes of one alien sound, one Orientalist construct. The Orientalist *net* incarcerating area studies on Asia as well as minorities of Asian ancestry becomes, paradoxically, the *nest* from which the crusade for Asian American selfhood is launched.

Some would denounce the notion of an Orientalist net as too Foucauldian and deterministic, which offers no way out of the discursive straitjacket. This is exactly the kind of charges leveled against *Orientalism*—that Said fails to demonstrate native and local oppositions to Orientalism. As I mentioned earlier, the alternative to the deathly embrace can be located in certain Nisei writers and, later in this book, in the textual pidgins of Louis Chu, Milton Murayama, and Wayne Wang. Nevertheless, this alternative is predicated on Asian Americans' willingness and capacity to erode the tyranny of the English language and of Americanization. With the monolingualism and assimilationism of a deathly embracer such as Amy Tan in Part III, there is little one can do to recuperate her novels from the abyss of Orientalism.

The full title of Kingston's 1976 novel is *The Woman Warrior: Memoirs of a Girlhood among Ghosts.* By pondering the meaning of "ghosts," one begins to appreciate Kingston's deconstructive, destabilizing text. "Ghosts" refer to white and black apparitions among whom the protagonist Maxine finds herself; they also refer to such Chinese phantoms as "No Name Woman" and "Sitting Ghost"; they further include candidates for membership in the crazed Moon Orchid and the superstitious Brave Orchid. Maxine the girl becomes the only human being groomed to be the woman warrior. Granted that the protagonist deflects the white gaze at "Orientals" through the litany of "Taxi Ghosts, Bus Ghosts, Police Ghosts, Fire Ghosts" and the like (113), the bulk of the novel, nevertheless, perpetuates a classic Orientalist strategy: glossing over the socioeconomic plight of aliens in our midst — immigrants such as Brave Orchid — while indulging in the mythic other of Fa Mu Lan and, to a lesser degree, of the barefoot doctor mother.

The cover design of the 1977 Vintage paperback edition of *The Woman Warrior* (figure 1) offers yet another vivid example of the interlocked Orientalist and ethnic impulses: a girl with long black hair and slant eyes is encircled by a fiery dragon, a trite marker for the Orient. The woman warrior cannot be visualized except through iconographic clichés. The book cover and promotional literature are, to be sure, the domain of the publisher, over which the author exercises little, if any, control. To this extent, my critique is directed toward the reception of Kingston as well as toward Kingston herself. For, after all, the book cover and the following pages are an integral whole, the fetishized dragon on the cover reemerging during the woman warrior's apprenticeship of the "dragon ways" of fighting (34). The crucial difference lies in the fact that although Kingston alludes to the intangibility of the legendary dragon — that one is never able to witness "a dragon whole" (35) — the cover simplifies and stylizes it. Kingston's best intentions are overshadowed by the popular taste for tropes within the reach of the human mind; furthermore, it is nearly impossible to sustain Kingston's Zen-like vision born out of an interdiction against envisioning.

Indeed, the dragon as a symbol illustrates perfectly the deathly embrace. The pages of this book are fraught with evidence of Asian Amer-

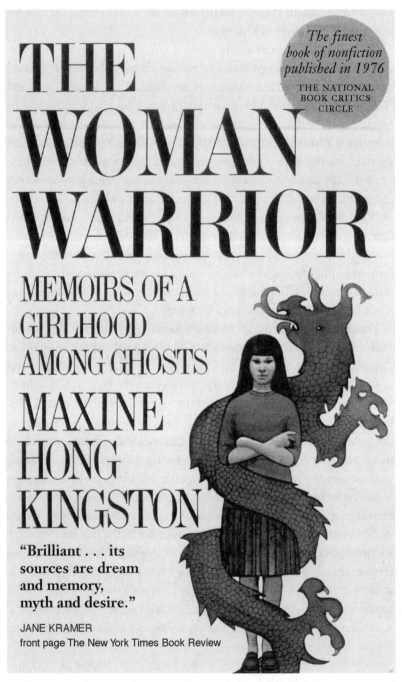

THE
WOMAN
WARRIOR

MEMOIRS OF A
GIRLHOOD
AMONG GHOSTS

MAXINE
HONG
KINGSTON

The finest book of nonfiction published in 1976

THE NATIONAL
BOOK CRITICS
CIRCLE

"Brilliant . . . its
sources are dream
and memory,
myth and desire."

JANE KRAMER
front page The New York Times Book Review

Figure 1. Cover of 1977 Vintage paperback edition of Maxine Hong Kingston's *The Woman Warrior*. Reprinted courtesy of Vintage Books, a division of Random House, Inc.

ican deployment of the dragon, notwithstanding the heavy exotic ambience of the creature in the West. An emblem of great ambiguity to Westerners, the dragon restlessly morphs from the godhead into a prehistoric beast, and back. The fetishization of dragons begins in chapter 1 with the characters of Emperor Ming and the Dragon Lady in the 1930s and 1940s comic strips. Bruce Lee's films discussed in chapter 3 frequently resort to dragons as nationalist icons. Vincent Chin in chapter 4 used to work at his father's Detroit restaurant called Golden Dragon. In chapters 5 and 6, Amy Tan gives both pictorial and verbal manifestations of dragons. Disney's *Mulan* (1998) in chapter 7 recycles relentlessly the mythic icon. In scholarly works, the symbol of dragon comes in handy as well, even though the critical thrust often does not bear on dragons at all. The cover of Sau-ling Cynthia Wong's *Reading Asian American Literature* presents two dragons entwined with the U.S. flag. Chapter 2 of Timothy P. Fong's *The First Suburban Chinatown: The Remaking of Monterey Park, California* (1994) is titled "Enter the Dragon: Economic Change," focusing on the sinologizing of the Los Angeles district as a result of the growth of the Pacific Rim economy and the influx of Taiwanese and Hong Kong businesses.

Ultimately, the dragon becomes a banal image, a stand-in for Asians and Asian Americans, in the same way that "Aiiieeeee!" is taken to be the quintessential alien expression. Both reflect the representational violence perpetrated against the silent other. Asian Americans, on the other hand, are also interpellated by the hegemonic ideology to the extent that they no longer perceive the interpellation. Moreover, a minority's survival in American society often hinges on exploiting rather than subverting stereotypes and banalities. Restaurants like Golden Dragon are found not only in Vincent Chin's Detroit but in almost every corner of the United States, serving primarily white customers with sweet and sour dishes and fortune cookies. When an Asian or Asian American learns to perform the deathly embrace well, they, the Americans, will come, amply illustrated by the following of Amy Tan and the box-office success of John Woo.

This book proceeds to interrogate the inextricability of Orientalism and Asian American ethnicity in four parts. Part I, "Clutch of Rape: Imperialist Adventure Narratives," opens with a chapter on the genre of adventure comic strips of the 1930s and 1940s, a visual representation of the Orient and the Oriental largely ignored today but unparalleled in its sway over the pre-television, Depression-tempered generations. Such comic strips as *Flash Gordon* and *Terry and the Pirates,* featuring contradictions of the evil Fu Manchu and the farcical, virtuous Charlie Chan (or their female counterparts of the Dragon Lady and Madame Butterfly), set up the naked prototype of Orientalist embrace: demonization and domestication of the other. The embrace amounts to an ideological choke hold, in which the Orientals strain for air. To demonstrate how pervasive and imperceptible this interpellation of Orientalist ideology is, chapter 2 focuses on Walt Disney's *Swiss Family Robinson* (1960). Disney's classic inherits the Robinsonade tradition of imperial exploits, while reflecting a heightened awareness of the danger looming in the East through the trope of Asian pirates. Precariously poised between the traditionalism of the 1950s and the turmoil of the 1960s, *Swiss Family Robinson* provides a glimpse at how family entertainment intersects with imperialist ideology in terms of the representation of nature, race, and gender.

Orientals as antagonists conceived in comic strips and demonized by Disney intensify their resistance around the globe and at the home front in the 1960s and 1970s. Part II, "Clash of Arms," examines the complex relationships between a trope of force and an identity, between martial metaphors and Asian America. Chapter 3 is a study of the popularization of Chinese martial arts via Bruce Lee during the warring 1970s, the duplication of martial images in originary Asian American literature such as *The Woman Warrior,* and the commodification of martial arts in American youth culture. Chapter 4 retraces a long-forgotten tragic consequence of the perception of a masculinized Asia—the murder of Vincent Chin. In chapter 3, the tumultuous international and U.S. domestic conditions of the 1970s are found to have necessitated the creation of a new image of the East in Bruce Lee (whose first name in Mandarin means "Little Dragon"), one grounded in the old stereotype of the Oriental's inhuman cruelty yet endeared to the public in the context of the civil rights movement and global changes. Lee's performance becomes a projection of, simultaneously, the volatile age and the mystical Orient. Echoing the chaotic times in their martial metaphors, Kingston and *Aiiieeeee!* seek to define the emerging Asian Americanness through its difference—neither Asian nor hegemonic American. But the gradual disappearance of martial metaphors in Asian American texts indicates a retreat from ethnic struggle, from infinite contestations and negations.

This chapter concludes with a look at the kaleidoscopic configurations of kung fu in American youth culture by focusing on the spawns of the video game *Mortal Kombat* in comic books, graphic novels, weekend cartoon shows on TV, toys, video arcades, and movie theaters. A real-life casualty of the "Fighting Chinaman" image was Vincent Chin, who was bludgeoned to death by two automobile factory workers with a baseball bat after a racial incident at a nude bar in Detroit in 1982. The assailants, originally sentenced to three years' probation and fined three thousand dollars, were acquitted in 1987. Chapter 4 interrogates the bashing of Chin against the sentiment of Japan bashing of the 1980s; it further explores the relationship between a murder and baseball, the national pastime/culture. The deathly embrace turns, sadly, literal in the Chin incident.

Both kinds of contemporary cultural practice in Parts III and IV arise from the previous decades, the ties best exemplified by the appeal of Bruce Lee. Lee's mystique derives from his ability to bring one of the pivotal symbols of ancient China into modern Western popular culture, to package martial arts in filmic language for moviegoers around the world. That ability stems yet again from Lee's familiarity with both the East and the West, both the minority condition in the United States and the postcolonial condition outside the United States. Lee's ambiguous opposition to and collusion with Orientalist images usher in the 1990s' twin phenomena of Part III, "Multicultural Flaunting of Ethnicity," and of Part IV, "Masquerading of Ethnicity." Asian American novelists such as Amy Tan in Part III compose as if having inherited the 1960s, yet Tan fetishizes ethnicity. On the other hand, global postcolonial writers such as the Anglo-Japanese Kazuo Ishiguro in Part IV proceed as if having graduated to a state of postethnicity, masking the minority complex in whiteface protagonists.

Part III turns first to recent developments of Asian American discourse, specifically Amy Tan's fictions. Growing out of the entanglements with Orientalism found in Kingston, Frank Chin, Bruce Lee, and other Asian Americans in the 1970s, this U.S.-born writer in the 1990s seems to have converted the utopian and activist spirit of the 1960s into a fashion, a stylization in ethnic writing. Chapter 5 on Amy Tan's *The Chinese Siamese Cat* contends that Tan is a new Orientalist who collaborates with the illustrator of her children's book in updating for our times the chinoiserie tradition and ethnic stereotypes of Chinese. Chapter 6 maintains, through a detailed analysis of *The Hundred Secret Senses* (1995), that Amy Tan of the 1990s continues the Orientalist strategies of the nineteenth century. What Tan offers is an "alternative" Orientalism, a New Age ethnicity mongrelized with primitivism, that appeals to Westerners' long-held Orientalist views of Asians and Asia under the guise of an embracing of ethnicity. This celebration of racial differences is further cast as a return to China's primordial, essentialist spirituality to heal a divided multiracial society and the atomized, reified postmodern selves. Tan's array of Orientalist clichés of interracial romance, Western missionaries, Chinese bandits, the Christianity-inspired Taiping Rebellion, framed by mixed-blood San Francisco yuppies and their comic, dog-like Chinese familiars with pidgin English, formulates exotic tales long cherished by Westerners. Chapter 7 on Disney's *Mulan* (1998) updates Orientalism in popular culture in the 1990s. Mulan and her 1990s siblings, all with suppressed family names, all by blood the children of Disney, are born out of multiculturalism. They serve to satisfy, at least superficially, the needs of the drastically changing demographics within the United States and elsewhere. Confronted with an ever-evolving global village, Disney resorts to polarized visions of the other to assuage the audience's sense of uncertainty. Bent upon re-orienting (pun intended), rather than dis-orienting, *Mulan* draws from Orientalist fantasies of yore, notwithstanding the inflections of contemporary youth culture.

Part IV contains only one chapter — chapter 8 on Kazuo Ishiguro. The fact that Ishiguro, an Anglo-Japanese writer whose career is launched by two "Japanese" novels, increasingly presents a tableau purged of Asianness suggests a need similar to Tan's. Suppressing his minority background enables him to be more British than the British. Ethnicity in either flaunting or masquerading becomes a performative act, a role-playing. Two minority writers — Tan and Ishiguro — embrace the hegemony in diverse poses, one presenting herself as the multicultural dance partner for the New Age ball, the other evacuating ethnicity for a union with the white hegemony.

My approach as a whole is interdisciplinary, encompassing Asian American, American, Asian, and postcolonial studies; it is multigeneric, drawing from fictions, essays, children's books, films, comics, video games, and court documents; it springs from the field of cultural studies where a social phenomenon is anatomized in all its complexities, regardless of the barriers between "high" and "popular" culture, adult and children's culture. Such a wide range of mediums constitutes an eclectic archive and demonstrates how Orientalism, an integral part of American culture, interpellates texts by Asian Americans and non-Asian Americans alike. Hence, comics by European American artists in early decades of the twentieth century, Disney movies of the 1960s and 1990s, Asian American texts then and now are equally imbued with this ideology. Indeed, without a panoramic view of American cultural productions spanning several decades, across racial and generic lines, one simply cannot perceive the choke hold that Orientalism maintains on the human mind. Some may quibble about the "Asian American" in the subtitle of this book because only a small number of non-Chinese American figures are featured — Kazuo Ishiguro, Peter Bacho, Sessue Hayakawa, and certain Nisei writers. But this book would be ill-served if I called it "Orientalism and *Chinese* American Identity." The deathly embrace affects or infects not just Chinese Americans, but Asian Americans, other minorities, and Americans in general. I elect to call all four types of embrace dea*th*ly rather than dea*d*ly for the added connotation of "deathly pale" or whiteness. Thus, ethnic identity atrophies in each point of contact because of its being wedded to the white hegemony. The paradox of deathly embrace brings out the love–hate relationship between Orientalism and Asian American identity, a stormy marriage with no end in sight.

Part I
Clutch of Rape
Imperialist Adventure Narratives

CHAPTER ONE

Imagining the Orient in the Golden Age of Adventure Comics

In 1995, the United States Postal Service put out a set of twenty gorgeously colored comic-strip classics stamps (figure 2). These stamps featured the most well known characters from the golden age of newspaper comic strips, roughly from the late 1920s to the 1930s, although major strips continued to enjoy popularity in the 1940s.[1] At the height of this genre in the 1930s, adventure comic strips, with the protagonists' daily heroic feats, boosted the sale of newspapers by offering diversion to Depression-weary Americans in the wake of the great stock market crash in 1929. Far more important than mere entertainment, adventure comic strips were, and still are, part of the stories a nation repeats to itself, out of which a national identity and myth arise. Of the twenty comic-strip classics selected by the postal service, Alex Gillespie Raymond's *Flash Gordon* and Milton Caniff's *Terry and the Pirates,* both begun in 1934, were credited with setting the standard for adventure comic strips (Harvey 124). To create tales of adventure, both strips included a supporting cast of "Orientals" in opposition to the American heroes. Moreover, *Terry* was set exclusively in the Orient. The only exception to *Terry*'s exotic locale was a sequence on March 23 and 24, 1946, when Terry's teenage assistant Hotshot Charlie was shown in his native Boston. What accounts for this shared Orientalist theme? What does this say about the American culture of those decades? Is there any legacy from a "lowbrow" art form that flourished half a century ago?

Before venturing to answer these questions, let us return to the postage stamps of *Flash* and *Terry,* for they are sanitized 1990s versions in terms of race and gender. A contrast with the archvillain Emperor Ming in *Flash* reveals that the postal Ming is made to lose his Oriental facial characteristics. He no longer sports goatees, slant eyes, and tapering fingernails; instead, a prominent Roman nose à la Marlon Brando stands out in profile. Similarly, the choice for the postal image for *Terry* is decidedly in favor of the wartime strips over the prewar ones. In the original comics, the adolescent Terry grew into a young air force pilot in the 1940s. With Terry's aviator jacket and the airplanes in the background in the stamp, one discerns no trace at all of the hero Pat Ryan, who adopted Terry in the strips of the 1930s, nor of the caricature of Chinese males (Connie the servant), nor of the exoticization of Chinese females (the vampress Dragon Lady). Moving away from the dashing Pat Ryan — "the handsome one," as the Dragon Lady called him — the postal service underlined the patriotic ethos of Terry the *pilot* over the horde of Chinese *pirates* associated with Pat's adventurous free-spiritedness. Such an act of cleansing was called for by the much-improved racial climate of the 1990s; to repeat the blatant racism in the strip would defeat the commercial purpose of the stamps based on the fin-de-siècle nostagia for a golden era. Nostalgia, nevertheless, is deceiving. These stamps evoke not only a yearning for a bygone era seemingly free from many of today's problems, they also conjure up an adolescent world of cartoon fantasy into which one escapes. The United States Postal Service has in effect purged the collective memory of adventure comic strips of the 1930s and 1940s, glossing over the dichotomized stereotypes of Orientals and the purportedly "virgin" continent explored/exploited by Western male characters.

This investigation thus opens with Depression-era xenophobia, which Sax Rohmer so successfully manipulates in the figure of Fu Manchu, whose image proliferates in popular culture, especially in the *Flash Gordon* comic strip with Ming the Merciless. Rohmer's oft-quoted admission that "I made my name on Fu Manchu because I know nothing about the Chinese . . . I do know something about Chinatown" (qtd. in Van Ash and Rohmer 72) signals the common thread of ignorance and discursive violence running through all the literature on the "Yellow Peril." Reacting to the rampant paranoia over the racial other, Earl Derr Biggers's comic detective Charlie Chan serves as, in William F. Wu's term, a psychological "overcompensation." The image of Chan manifests itself in the bucktoothed, slant-eyed, protruding-eared, English-mangling Chinese domestic Connie in *Terry and the Pirates* of the thirties and forties, which also features the Dragon Lady. The obsession of the Dragon Lady and of her counterparts in other comics for the American hero maps out a narcissistic and imperialist masculinity at the heart of the culture that engendered the golden age of comics. Constructed in the absence of any resistance from the ethnic other, Ming and Connie (or the Dragon Lady and Madame Butterfly) bespeak the schizophrenia within the West, which projects its dualistic impulses of fear and romance, of repulsion and attraction onto the "Yellow Peril" and its comic relief.

Comic strips were surely not the only medium of the period through which American culture expressed its desires. A cursory glance at Hollywood films of the 1930s reveals numerous productions featuring a sinister Fu Manchu, or a mysterious Chinese figure: *The Mask of Manchu* (1932), *The Hachet Man* (1932), *Limehouse Blue* (1934), *The Mysterious Mr. Wong* (1935), *Chinatown Squad* (1935), *She* (1935), *China Seas* (1935), *Secret Agent* (1936), *Lost Horizon* (1937), *The Soldier and the Lady* (1937), *China Passage* (1937), and *Shadows of the Orient* (1937). But adventure comic strips remain a largely ignored yet immensely important source of visual representations of Orientals for pretelevision generations. Especially for the generation that endured the Depression, comics countered, in a manner of speaking, colossal tragedies. The coming of age of comics in the late 1920s did not coincide by chance with the crash and the ensuing Depression; comics were conceived, literally, by the Depression.

When one is deprived of bread, to rephrase the advice of wise Roman emperors, circus is the next best thing, since a circus provides adventures to escape from, and scapegoats to rationalize, people's misery. For instance, English stories of adventure from the 1870s to World War I, observed Robert Dixon, served as "an antidote to the [alleged] degeneration and feminising of the race" through "their accessible fantasy of masculine and Anglo-Saxon supremacy in a world turned upside down" (5). In general, adventures, real or imagined, assisted in empire and character building. Commenting on the intersection of the British Empire and yarns of adventure, Martin Green maintained that "the adventure tales that formed the light reading of Englishmen for two hundred years and more after *Robinson Crusoe* were, in fact, the energizing myth of English imperialism" (3). Green further dated the rise of the British Empire around the time of "the Union of England with Scotland, in 1707," which corresponded to "the very historical moment when the adventure tale began to be written, since *Robinson Crusoe* appeared in 1719" (5).

Adventure tales were invaluable in perpetuating not only a national myth but a masculine myth, the two invariably intertwined in patriarchal cultures. Joseph Bristow wrote that "it was the duty of boys' narratives to suture . . . discrete elements that . . . made the hero an agent of moral restraint, on the one hand, and the embodiment of intrepid exploration on the other" (qtd. in Dixon 3). In the case of adventure comic strips, the shortest route from boyhood to a "moral" and "intrepid" adulthood seemed to cut across the exotic terrain of China and the erotic body of Chinese females. Sexuality, of course, has always played a crucial role in the growing pains of adolescents. Patricia Meyer Spacks designated adolescence as "the time of life when the individual has developed full sexual capacity but has not yet assumed a full adult role in society" (7). An ambivalent form of human expression, comic strips of the 1930s and 1940s articulated the equally ambivalent desires of adolescence, either those minors living it or those elders reliving it. A hidden male lineage whereby one generation instilled ideology in the next, comics were suspended between childhood and adulthood, between "low" and "high" art, between fantasy of power and reality of powerlessness, between the extremities and the very soul of a culture, between boys who indulged in comic strips and their fathers who purchased the newspaper for, supposedly, more serious motives. As such, the pulpy nature of action-packed adventure strips was the essence of their existence and propagation. Like James Bond films, adventure strips thrived on incidents, each stunt soon forgotten so that another could be performed. The repetition of action was predicated on the paradox of instant gratification and ever-deepening thirst. A Tantalus given briny water, adventure strips satiated only to further dehydrate the consumer, hence making possible endless reruns of similar events.

Emperor Ming and His Mongolian Horde

The creator of *Flash Gordon*, Alex Gillespie Raymond, took up illustration because he became unemployed in the Great Depression. Raymond drew the strips from 1934 to 1944, the year when he was commissioned a captain in the Marine Corps Reserve.[2] After the war, he stopped *Flash* and began the detective strip *Rip Kirby*. He was killed in an auto accident in 1956. Despite its sci-fi, futuristic subject matter and style, *Flash* mirrored the hardships of its time. The Depression not only accounted for the convergence of an out-of-work artist and his economically strained fans in stories of escapades, but it also explained the apocalyptic obsession in science fiction of that period. Industrialization, which created the dominance of the West in modern times, might have, Americans wondered, run amok. The fear of the overheated economy and technology was best dramatized in the panic caused by Orson Welles's radio broadcast of the invasion from Mars on October 30, 1938. Therefore, the opening episode of *Flash* in the Sunday newspapers on January 7, 1934, depicted a catastrophe by which the world would come to an end. A planet was on a collision course with the Earth. A mad scientist, Dr. Zarkov, kidnapped Flash and his girlfriend Dale Arden in a spaceship designed to crash against the planet and save the world. The spaceship landed on the planet instead, which turned out to be Mongo, ruled by Ming the Merciless. Mongo punned with Mongol, evoking the medieval fear of Genghis Khan, which had fueled the phobia of the "Yellow Peril" in the United States since the nineteenth century.[3] Thus the *Flash* saga unfolded in a land replete with prehistoric dinosaurs, Stone Age men, medieval castles, and futuristic spaceships and weaponry. Born out of a paranoia of civilization about to collapse, the decade-long epic was sustained by, among others, the prime mover of all evil on Mongo and elsewhere—the yellow man.

Indeed, despite phantasmogoric episodes of Hawkmen, Shark Men, Death Dwarves, Lionmen, Tuskmen, Dragonmen, Cliff Men, Fire People, Blue Magic Men, Red Monkeymen, Roman gladiators butchering one another in stadiums, despite technological gadgets of spaceships, poison gas, eletrocution manacles, ray guns, these were but mere ripples, chain reactions from a cancerous core, which was inhabited solely by Chinese, or rather, constructs allegedly Chinese. Blessed by the god Tao, Ming commanded a loyal legion composed of Captain Lin Chu, Captain Lunging, Captain Luong, Admiral Chiung, and other functionaries with concocted Chinese names. The demonization of Orientals was of course the shared theme of literature of the "Yellow Peril," to which *Flash Gordon* belonged. William F. Wu defined the "Yellow Peril" as

the threat to the United States that some white American authors believed was posed by the people of East Asia. As a literary theme, the fear of this threat focused on specific issues, including possible military invasion from Asia, perceived competition to the white labor force from

Asian workers, the alleged moral degeneracy of Asian people, and the potential genetic mixing of Anglo-Saxons with Asians, who were considered a biologically inferior race. (1)

Wu tied the Yellow Peril to national and international events: immigration of Asians to the United States, the Boxer Rebellion, annexation of the Philippines by the United States, Japan's victory in the Russo-Japanese War of 1905–6, and the subsequent Japanese expansion (3).

In literature, the West's anxiety festered into the grotesque Fu Manchu in Sax Rohmer's mysteries from 1913 until the author's death in 1959. Rohmer wrote a total of thirteen novels, three short stories, and one novelette. Ming the Merciless descended from this tradition of Fu Manchu. Rohmer saw the early decades of the twentieth century as a propitious moment for "launching a Chinese villain on the market," because of the 1900 anti-foreign Boxer Rebellion in China and contemporaneous seedy events in Limehouse, London's erstwhile Chinatown (qtd. in Van Ash and Rohmer 75). The obfuscation of China and Chinatown in this quote and in Rohmer's admission cited earlier ("I know nothing about the Chinese . . . I do know something about the Chinatown") epitomized the hegemonic terrorism in categorizing aliens at will and assigning whatever characteristics to them.

Fu Manchu was most significant as a literary figure in that he provided a heretofore missing ruler image for all the negative stereotypes of the Chinese. All the bungling, silly, infiltrating Chinese were group representations, but Fu furnished a quintessential image to combine all the stereotypes. "Fu Manchu fills a power vacuum," hypothesized Wu, "that had existed in the tales of Chinese immigration and infiltration; with his presence as 'the yellow peril' incarnate" (173). This was clearly the case in *Flash,* where the cold intellect and evil genius of Ming the Merciless poised to take over the world. Even the visual image of Emperor Ming stemmed from Fu Manchu. To represent Fu Manchu, a Satan beyond this mundane world of ours, Rohmer appealed to readers' power to fantasize:

> Imagine a person, tall, lean and feline, high-shouldered, with a brow like Shakespeare and a face like Satan, a close-shaven skull, and long, magnetic eyes of the true cat-green. Invest him with all the cruel cunning of an entire Eastern race, accumulated in one giant intellect, and with all the resources of science past and present, with all the resources, if you will, of a wealthy government — which, however, already has denied all

knowledge of his existence. Imagine that awful being, and you have a
mental picture of Dr. Fu-Manchu, the yellow peril incarnate in one man.
(*The Mystery of Dr. Fu Manchu* 19)

Rohmer dropped the hyphen in "Fu-Manchu" after the first three novels.
In addition to imagining the unimaginable, because Fu Manchu did not
exist other than in people's mind, Rohmer's exhortation blended animalistic otherness and parts of oneself. Fu was said to possess many bestial
characteristics, while having Shakespeare's intelligence, an education at
a Western university, and knowledge of modern Western science. The
comparison to Satan, the fallen archangel, proved that the Bible contributed an amazing amount of images and vocabulary whereby the
Asian other, especially the prominent ones like Raymond's Emperor Ming
and Caniff's the Dragon Lady, was represented. Consider the archaic,
quasi-King James speech of these Asian characters. The Dragon Lady
called Terry "the blond one"; her expendable followers were "the low-
born ones." Such addresses harked back to the refrains in the Bible and
the voluminous literature it had inspired, such as the "firstborn" (Exod.
12:29), "the One in Heaven," and more.

The Oriental other, as a consequence, turned out to be projections of
the Euro-American self. The astuteness of Fu was personified by Shakespeare and scientific knowledge, the part of its accomplishment much
flaunted by the West. The dark side of Fu — embodied in his "catlike"
gait, his "reptilian gaze" (105), culminating in his Mephistophelian
power — is associated with the animalistic, inhuman evil long despised
by, but still a part of, the West.

With regard to the iconography of Ming the Merciless, Raymond inherited Rohmer's description of Fu Manchu, touches of the artist's own
imagination notwithstanding. In the beginning of his long reign, Ming
resembled a Roman general, with a Roman helmet and armors, two
strong legs, his arm outstretched in a military salute (figure 3). But even
in this early metamorphosis, Ming was after all *Ming*, unmistakably "Oriental" in terms of his facial traits, especially the goatees. Moreover, his
breastplate bore the coat of arms of a serpentine dragon, the beast closely
linked with China. As Raymond experimented with the medium, Emperor Ming came to acquire all the stereotypical markings of the evil
Chinaman: garbed in a long robe often decorated with dragons, his head
shaved or sporting a cap with a dragon, long and thin goatees, eyes half-

closed or slantingly drawn, and, at times, long fingernails and pointed ears (figures 4 and 5).

Pitted against this pictorialization of a vicious alien was the hero Flash Gordon, the paragon of American masculinity, blond, muscular, Waspish, steadfast, and chaste. A Yale graduate and world-class polo player, Flash was so imbued with American puritanism that he exhibited an incredible innocence of Aura's (Emperor Ming's daughter) carnal interest in him (Barshay 5). In a series of films in the 1930s based on the comic strip, Larry "Buster" Crabbe was selected for the role of Flash as a result of his resemblance to the comic-strip character, which was in turn based on the stereotype of the "All-American" athlete. Crabbe was the Olympic freestyle swimming champion of 1932, strikingly Aryan with his hair dyed blond (Barshay 4).

Flash Gordon's British ancestors, the impulsive detective Denis Nayland Smith and his sidekick Dr. Petrie, were not as good-looking in the hands of Sax Rohmer. Whereas mysteries depended on the fast-paced plot to attract adult readers, comics catered to adolescents' or adolescent-like craving for glamorization, physically embodied in heroes and heroines. The impact of illustration and advertisement on the human figures in adventure strips was also enormous. Most female characters in Alex Gillespie Raymond and Milton Caniff seemed to have stepped right out of a New York fashion show. Dale Arden at one point of the story was supposedly in disguise to rescue Flash (figure 6), but Dale's profile reminded one of the fashion of the 1930s with the wide-brimmed hat and frills around the neck. Whether in a rescue attempt or to be rescued by Flash, females surrounding the hero served a function much like that of Oriental antagonists. Only by means of an opposition to aliens, on the one hand, and a perpetual deferment of consummation with women, on the other, could the hero tower over the few panels in the daily newspaper.

All the women in Flash's career silhouetted, once again, the "internal drama" of the West. Fu Manchu and Ming the Merciless were inscribed both with the blessed and the cursed traits of the West because they were the West's own shadows. In the attempt of dissociation, the West gave them Asian names and appearances. Similarly, all the female enemy aliens the heroes fraternized with were Eurasian or Eurasian-looking. This phenomenon extended beyond comic strips to Hollywood movies and fiction, beyond the 1930s to the present. The rationale seemed to be that to be compatible with Caucasian males, females ought to have obtained traits of the "superior" race — taller, fairer skin color, higher nose ridge, and whatnot. Furthermore, it was a commercial consideration, since few American moviegoers or fiction readers would regard the stereotypical Oriental face — broad and flat — as bewitchingly beautiful. Yet the Eurasian protagonists should also display a touch of the exotic Orient in, for instance, their slant eyes and long black hair, in part to justify the Oriental feminine qualities — the geisha's submissiveness and sensuousness — to massage the male ego.

As such, Fu Manchu's daughter Fah Lo Suee ("Sweet Perfume"), who appeared in *Daughter of Fu Manchu* (1931), had a Russian mother, endowing her with attractive Caucasian characteristics, yet a questionable character due in part to the mother's racial origin. Displaying love at first sight toward Dr. Petrie, Fu Manchu's slave-assassin Kâramanèh exhibited signs of hybridization as well: "With the skin of a perfect blonde, she had eyes and lashes as black as a creole's" (15). Kâramanèh risked her own life to save Dr. Petrie on a number of occasions, testifying to her total devotion, which was not repaid by her benefactor, other than some fleeting thoughts. The Anglo-American masculinity constructed by Rohmer via his protagonists and condoned by Rohmer's fans was grounded on the drive for domination rather than on love and giving. The worst manifestation of this male chauvinism surfaced in Nayland Smith's advice to Petrie, one constituting a classic case of the rape mentality: "If you would only seize her by the hair, drag her to some cellar, hurl her down, and stand over her with a whip, she would tell you everything she knows . . . And she would adore you for your savagery, deeming your [*sic*] forceful and strong!" (96). Familiar rings of this piece of advice to Petrie and to the readers resounded throughout adventure comic strips.

Just as Kâramanèh helped Petrie and Smith escape from the clutches of her master, Aura assisted Flash in eluding her own father, Emperor Ming. Physically, the interracial Aura and the Caucasian Dale Arden resembled each other (figure 7). Without the help of the balloons, the reader would fail to distinguish between the two females in bondage in the two panels of figure 7. In fact, Aura was more of a brunette than Dale, who had black hair. The Caucasian lineage of Kâramanèh and Aura pulled them toward the magnet of white heroes over their duty to Oriental patriarchs. Their love for the heroes, nonetheless, must remain unrequited because their "impure" bloodline and excessive sensuality doomed them to the role of mistress or lover—totally spurned in the case of Aura. Symptomatic of the colonialist mentality, the hero's love was reserved for his equals—Caucasian heroines such as Dale Arden.

Connie and Big Stoop; the Dragon Lady and Miss Lace

A pivotal change came over *Flash Gordon* in the 1940s: Emperor Ming vanished like a casualty of war. Ming the Merciless and his Mongolian horde, all vaguely Chinese, had probably gone out of style in World War II when China became the United States' ally. Such was the fate of extremely demonic images of Fu Manchu and Ming. Rohmer's mysteries and Raymond's prewar strip required a distant, if not hostile, relationship between their fans and China. The attack of Pearl Harbor on December 7, 1941, changed everything. Another comic strip featuring Chinese and China, however, survived long after the war. Milton Caniff's *Terry and the Pirates* relied on more realistic, yet still highly Orientalized, setting and characters than Raymond's futuristic project.[4] *Terry*, furthermore, was placed squarely in China, making a transition to wartime events relatively effortless. A year after the war, Caniff stopped drawing *Terry*, but the strips were carried on by other artists until 1973, as the back of the *Terry* postage stamp indicated. Even in the late 1990s, *Terry and the Pirates* was revived by newspaper syndicates across the country.

In an exhibition at the Museum of Cartoon Art in 1985, Milton Caniff was honored as the "Rembrandt of Comic Strips." Caniff, who died at the age of eighty-one three years later, introduced high artistic standards into the profession in his career over half a century. The key to the longevity of Caniff's Chinese characters, compared to the short-lived Ming, lay in the illustrator's adherence to an opposite tradition in Orientalism: the anti-Fu Manchu, or the clownish, harmless Charlie Chan. William F. Wu argued that the two stereotypes did not represent "archetypal dualities" of good versus evil, or of crime versus law, but racial dualities, "yellow versus white, with Fu Manchu embodying yellow power and Charlie Chan supporting white supremacy" (164). Wu insightfully diagnosed the Chinese Hawaiian detective Chan as his creator Earl Derr Biggers's "overcompensation . . . to break away from the Yellow Peril" (176) in six mysteries between 1925 and 1932, ending with Biggers's death in 1933. Whether overcompensation or not, the Chinese twins must somehow coexist, as Fu Manchu alone presented too much of a threat to the collective psyche. Even while the Depression lingered on and while *Flash*

Gordon spawned the evil Chinaman, the genre of comic strips brought forth its own antithesis of Fu Manchu. Alfred Andriola was handpicked by Biggers to do the Charlie Chan comic strips, which ran from 1935 to 1938. Andriola's detective, it is worthwhile noting, worked for world peace.

By casting Chan as a mixed-blood at "a halfway point to Asia" (Wu 174), by allowing Chan to rise from a houseboy in Hawaii to a middle-class detective working for Caucasian clients, Biggers anticipated the model minority argument decades later. His upward mobility was implied to result from cultural, if not genealogical, amalgamation with the superior race. Iconographically, Chan came through as the reverse of Fu: "The villain is tall, bony, and yellow; the detective is shorter, chubby, and pink. The former is angry and threatening; the latter stays calm and apologetic. Fu Manchu speaks precise, accurate English; Charlie Chan speaks in broken English with incorrect grammar. Fu represents his race; his counterpart stands away from the other Asian Hawaiians" (Wu 180–81). Yet Wu cautioned against a total separation of the twins: "That Charlie Chan had been tamed, however, implies that he conceivably could have been wild, or uncontrolled, and so he is a reflection of the Yellow Peril though not a part of it" (182). Even the images of Fu and Chan might not be as polarized as Wu suggested. As spotty as Charlie Chan's two goatees were, he nevertheless had them, just like Fu Manchu.

Although Caniff also presented a wide array of vile Chinese characters, none of them came close to the grandeur of Fu Manchu. Caniff's major contributions to Orientalism were Connie and Big Stoop, descendants of the Chan clan, so to speak, and the Dragon Lady, the opposite image of Madame Butterfly. Despite the differences between Fu Manchu and his Oriental counterparts in *Terry*, Caniff's explication of his ties to Chinese materials betrayed a Rohmeresque arrogance: "I have never been to China, so I go to the next best place, the Public Library . . . For authentic speech mannerisms I plow through a pile of books by traveled people from Pearl Buck to Noël Coward. By now I am an arm-chair Marco Polo and tipping my hat to every Chinese laundryman in New York" (qtd. in Maurice Horn's Introduction to *Terry and the Pirates: China Journey*). Caniff eagerly identified himself with Orientalist forebears—Marco Polo, Noël Coward, Pearl Buck, and the Oriental collection at the New York Public Library. The fabricated pidgin English in Buck, Coward, and other more flagrant perpetrators was deemed "authentic speech mannerisms" for Connie et al. Finally, like Rohmer's indebtedness to Limehouse, Caniff credited Chinese laundrymen in New York for stimulating his work.

Caniff in "Terry, the Pirates and I," Preface to *Terry and the Pirates: China Journey,* reported his intention: "From the start in TERRY the thrust was to grab the reader who thought he led a dull life and longed for the exotic charms of the Orient." Whereas *Flash Gordon* opened with an apocalyptic vision of civilization coming to an end, *Terry* initiated its Depression-era readers into the exotic Orient. The teenage Terry Lee and his "pal" or father figure, Pat Ryan, led the comic strip's fans on a treasure hunt up the river along China's coast for the cache of wealth left buried by Terry's grandfather. A Conradian journey devoid of night-marish transformations, it remained bitterly ironic that while Chinese had joined the gold rush to California in the mid-nineteenth century, and while San Francisco continues to be called "Old Gold Mountain" in Mandarin today, Americans imagined gold hunting in China.

Pat and Terry retained the service of a Chinese boy, Connie, short for George Webster Confucius, to facilitate their search. A feminine nick-name conferred by his white masters who shortened and belittled the name "Confucius," "Connie" punned with "cunning." In the evolution of the strip, Connie graduated from a cook and porter to the protagonists' confidant, but his fundamental inferiority and marginality never varied. Out of the tableau of Chinese characters, most of whom were unnamed, indistinguishable bandits, commoners, and victims, Connie, as distorted as he was, grew in stature, if only for his consistent presence. But even an avid Caniffite would be hard-pressed to describe Connie's character other than in stereotypical terms such as devoted and farcical. Nor could he or she do much to recuperate Connie's physical characteristics beyond his stereotypical features: a bald head, a blank and dumb face, buckteeth, slant eyes, giant ears, in a tuxedo with tails or a Chinese-style long robe, and white gloves, the last of which reminds one of the costume for Mickey Mouse and blackface performance (figure 8).

To create Connie, Caniff may have borrowed from the originary image of newspaper comic strips, Richard F. Outcault's Yellow Kid, which ran from 1895 to 1898 (figure 9 and the first postage stamp in figure 2). Figure 9 was an earlier image drawn by Outcault himself and had, in Joyce Mil-ton's words, "vaguely Asian features" (41), particularly in view of the fact that the scribblings or folds on the lower half of the Kid's robe or nightshirt looked like strokes of Chinese ideograms. Outcault had identified the Yellow Kid, in spite of the obvious association with the Yellow Peril around 1900, as a poor child from an Irish immigrant family in Hogan's Alley. But the physical resemblance between the Yellow Kid and Connie was too striking to be ignored—bald head, protruding ears, beady eyes, and buckteeth. Robert C. Harvey likewise described the Yellow Kid as having a "vaguely Oriental visage baring its two front teeth at the reader in a grin at once vacuous and knowing" (6), which was a perfect portrayal of Connie's expression dominated by the buckteeth. Even if the Yellow Kid were indeed an archetype in Outcault's works, the yellow kid Connie in Caniff was unmistakably stereotypical, with all the Charlie Chan Orientalist trappings to render him ludicrous. Caniff's revisioning, if not inheriting, of the comics' legacy of ethnic caricatures, which could be traced back to the earliest newspaper strips in New York by Outcault, intimated an inherent bent of comics art. This proclivity manifested itself in the golden age of adventure comic strips as well, in characters such as the ones explored in this book.

Connie was even more elusive to the reader because his pidgin English, so fragmentary and disjointed, dictated a perfunctory skimming of his lines for comic relief. Any serious perusal of Connie's words would produce no discernible pattern of speech. Until a grammar of Connie's pidgin English fabricated by Westerners for Westerners might be compiled, one must be content to leave Connie's strange lingo to the realm of racist distortions. With his verbosity making no sense, Connie was de facto mute. On the other hand, Big Stoop, a giant whose tongue was cut out by the Dragon Lady, was truly voiceless. Big Stoop extended Connie's domestic image into one of faithful, uncomplaining beast of burden (figure 10). Figure 10 bears out the irony that although Big Stoop towered over and swooped up Terry, his nickname as well as his role subjugated him to the protagonists.

It is the strange logic of our world that simply by making cameo appearances a superstar, in art or in life, should outshine the supporting cast, treated as little more than background props. Caniff's true achievement in Orientalist characterization lay not in the likes of Connie or Big Stoop but in the Dragon Lady, who wove in and out of the strip for a decade. The former group constituted merely comic relief, whereas the Dragon Lady was an antagonist the heroes must reckon with. Consistent with Raymond's erotic fantasy to forge Western masculinity, the Eurasian-looking Dragon Lady was infatuated with the hero Pat Ryan in the 1930s, and increasingly with the matured Terry Lee in the 1940s. (The Dragon Lady, needless to say, never aged throughout the strips.) Hence, her viciousness toward others only accentuated her abandoned obsession with the American protagonists.

Onto the curvaceous body of the Dragon Lady the West projected its morbid narcissism. Fu Manchu's sadism and Charlie Chan's loyalty were fused and feminized in her, and she became a mere girl, vulnerable and vindictive, in the presence of the irresistible Pat Ryan. Examples of the emotional entanglement between Pat Ryan and the Dragon Lady abounded whenever the Dragon Lady graced the strip. In a 1935 episode (figure 11), Pat, Terry, and Connie were prisoners of the Dragon Lady, who introduced them to her torture chamber. True to her name, the back of her dress displayed a curled dark dragon. True to caricature, all her Chinese pirates looked subhuman, almost apelike. The instruments of torture she relished in describing — the boiling oil, the millstone that ground from the feet up, and many more in subsequent panels — were followed in the next installment of the strip by the hostess Dragon Lady entertaining Pat and Terry with delicious Chinese cuisine (figure 12). Her guests, nevertheless, declined the exotic dishes she deigned to serve herself. The femme fatale who devoured men sadistically turned into a solicitous geisha, conquered by the power of love for a white male. Even the characters' kneeling posture at the low table derived from Japanese rather than Chinese table manners of the time.

Although the Dragon Lady's ambivalent character came through verbal description in the preceding example, the next one, also in 1935, did it by means of the trademark of adventure comic strips — action (figure 13). The Dragon Lady is seen disposing of her enemies, while an unconscious Pat lies on the couch. The blank background directs the reader's attention to the fighting. The final or gag panel shows the Dragon Lady reclining on her chair and playing a pi-pa (Chinese lute) to greet Pat as he gradually comes to. Yet the exemplary set of panels exuding sexual tension between the protagonists was that of October 18, 1936 (figure 14). Via food or cannibalistic metaphors, the repartee of a Pat in handcuffs and the Dragon Lady with a cigarette dangling from her mouth was tantamount to the bickering between two lovers. While feeding her prisoner, the Dragon Lady spoke of starving or nibbling him alive, attesting to her urge to overpower him, a "pet chimpanzee." Yet Pat, with whom the fans identified, remained utterly naive to her designs. Pat confessed his igorance as to the Dragon Lady's motives in capturing him, joking of suing her, and describing her as a "shy little Oriental maid with a disposition like a Gila monster." Pat acted rather as an innocent flirt to aggrandize male readers' ego: despite the withholding of love by the male, his admirer expressed passionate sentiments in possessive and cannibalist language. By sexually remaining pure and out of reach, the body of Pat Ryan and the white masculinity he symbolized dominated the adventure comic strip. The intensity and imbalance of power in this set of panels was further pictorialized in the unsteady, skewed scene on a junk. Caniff varied camera angles in every panel, a long shot from the ocean alternating with a medium shot through the junk's window. The window and the railing panels were horizontally divided by a tilting line, either the window sill or the wooden railing itself, thus enacting the fluctuating, volatile human relationship.

With all the ruthlessness of the Dragon Lady, an episode in 1936 (figure 15) brought to mind the rape mentality vis-à-vis the Orient(al) ingrained in literature of this kind, ranging from Nayland Smith's advice in *The Mystery of Fu Manchu* to Pat Ryan's strong-arm tactic. Pat discovered that in the attempt to coerce him to join her crime ring, the Dragon Lady made him draw lots from three slips, all written "join." An exposed Dragon Lady was seen physically vanquished, leaning on the floor, while Pat, despite his right arm in a sling, stood upright and barked commands at her: "From now on you take orders from ME!!... You asked for it!—I'm going to break you—and you're goin' to LIKE IT!!" Yet Pat was the one with a broken arm. The gag panel further offered a twist to this Orientalist, masculinist formula. As Pat and Terry exited the room, the caption read: "...the Dragon Lady instead of being angry, gazes after them, and smiles..." Assuredly, the enigmatic smile stemmed from a source no less Orientalist and masculinist. The Dragon Lady triumphed through feminine guiles: Pat had been won over by a trick within a trick, made to believe that he had succeeded in exposing her hoax. A rare moment in the strips when the Dragon Lady remained almost entirely reticent for the duration of the daily installment, her silent grin would be taken, by any male reader, to suggest that she indeed enjoyed being overwhelmed by men.

Like so many other incredible episodes, the Dragon Lady never grew old and eventually became a compatible rival, in war and in love, with Terry, who joined the war against the Japanese as a pilot. In these strips in the 1940s, Terry's adolescent role was replaced by Hotshot Charlie. An episode in 1946 displayed a wounded Dragon Lady, rescued by Terry and now resting in his airplane (figure 16). The conversation implied an age difference (Pat never called her "ma'am"), but not one so great as to render her interest in the "golden one" as maternal love. The intimacy on a rickety airplane between a tenderfoot and his injured passenger — of his reaching over to loosen her safety belt, of her stroking dangerously close to his earlobe, and of her desire to kiss him — approximated the erotic energy seen years before on a bobbing junk between a male in shackles and a female emotionally shackled.

From 1942 to 1946, concurrent with the production of *Terry and the Pirates*, Caniff volunteered to draw, for the Camp Newspaper Service, *Male Call*, a continuity comic strip to be serialized over a period of time. The service's publications were distributed to military personnel, especially soldiers fighting overseas. Like *Terry*, *Male Call* evidenced Caniff's and his male readers' nationalist and masculinist desires via an eroticization of the Orient. *Male Call* was printed in the military press and reached a syndication of three thousand newspapers and some fifteen million servicemen and countless civilians to boot (Bill Mauldin's Preface to Caniff, *Male Call* 7). Labeled "an aviation buff and devout patriot" by Mauldin (6), Caniff volunteered his service out of a sense of guilt. As if to justify his wartime civilian status, Caniff wrote in "The Two-minute Furlough" that he contracted phlebitis from an insect bite in the 1920s and could not pass the physicals to join the military a number of times (*Male Call* 9). Caniff's pre–*Male Call* war effort thus began with a poster for the National Defense on "what happened if we were bombed" (9), which was distributed on the West Coast the day after Pearl Harbor. His next assignment was to design posters warning against venereal disease, or rather, advertising the use of condoms. Being such a fine artist, his female characters attracted considerably more attention than the message. Caniff's art had invariably intersected with sexuality, but *Male Call* exemplified the Orientalist formulation of white masculinity.

When he embarked on the comic strip for the Camp Newspaper Service, Caniff initially borrowed the title of his *Terry and the Pirates* and featured Burma, the all-American blonde out of the adventure strip, amid American GIs. This ran from October 11, 1942, to January 10, 1943, followed by *Male Call* centered on a vaguely Oriental woman, Miss Lace, from January 24, 1943, to the end of 1946. The specific weekly sequence that was blocked by the military was "Solid Sender" (figure 17), which Caniff reinked as the inaugural strip for *Male Call*, changing Burma into Miss Lace (figure 18). The metamorphosis was a crucial one, ensuring the strip's popularity while dodging ethical and political censorship. The military's intervention probably alerted Caniff to the inherent problem of his initial productions: "I didn't use the *Terry* characters, but the people in it were obviously right out of the strip, including the bad girls" (9). Caniff must have realized that the tease Burma, despite her name, was perilously similar to GIs' sweethearts, real or imagined, back in the United States, and hence threatened to demolish their male fantasy of possessing both alluring mistresses such as Aura, Kâramanèh, and the Dragon Lady, on the one hand, and a faithful American wife awaiting their return, on the other. Having miscalculated in merging the wife with the mistress, Caniff moved to distance Miss Lace from the blonde Burma. Closer now to the prototype of the Eurasian Dragon Lady, Miss Lace was also given a feminine rather than an Oriental name.

Regardless of such tinkerings, the strip of August 22, 1943, proved Miss Lace's identity as an "easygoing" foreign woman (figure 19). In an exotic location of low walls with tiles, Miss Lace nestled toward the soldier, euphemistically called "General," dictating a love letter to his "sugar" back home. Caniff further intimated the race of Miss Lace in terms of her dark, straight hair, her surroundings of Chinese buildings and a statuette of Buddha (September 19, 1943), and her homely Chinese servants speaking pidgin English, a scene frequently found between the Dragon Lady and her maids (March 26, 1944, and October 15, 1944). During the cold war, various strands of Caniff's Orientalism survived in *Steve Canyon* in the 1950s, with its exotic Chinese princess and Miss Calhoun, the tycoon who resembles the Dragon Lady in temperament and in appearance. Even though Miss Lace the wartime companion and other creations of Caniff's may have been forgotten by the majority of Americans, the Orientalist reign that adventure comic strips enjoyed at one time was succeeded by that of film, advertising, television, and popular culture in subsequent decades.

Within the genre of comic strips, Fu Manchu was revived in the 1970s and 1980s by Marvel Comics as *The Hands of Shang-chi, Master of Kung Fu* (figures 20 and 21). The interracial child of Fu Manchu and a Russian woman, Shang-chi is modeled after Bruce Lee. Marvel Comics also brought out six issues of *Bruce Lee* in 1994. In addition to the image of kung fu master, the representation of Orientals as mad scientists continues to dominate. The facade of science for Rohmer's Fu Manchu develops into the sci-fi characteristic of Raymond's Emperor Ming, both betraying the Western anxiety over industrial growth. Another Marvel Comics strip contemporaneous with *Shang-chi* is *Dr. Strange.* Granted that this scientist is not particularly Oriental, there exist many Oriental touches, such as Dr. Stephen Strange's servant Wong and Wong's skeletal lover Xaos. The temptation to duplicate Oriental villains is simply too great to resist even in recent mainstream Hollywood productions. In the film versions of *Star Trek* alone, evil is located in Khan (played by Ricardo Montalban) in *Star Trek II: The Wrath of Khan* (1982) and in General Chan (played by Christopher Plummer) in *Star Trek VI: The Undiscovered Country* (1991). While Captain Kirk and Mr. Spock may boldly go where no one has gone before in the capitalist *Enterprise,* they seem to carry the age-old cartoonish prejudices about the Orient.

Figure 2. United States Postal Service comic-strip Classic Collection stamps. Note, in particular, *Flash Gordon* and *Terry and the Pirates*.

Figure 3. *Flash Gordon*: Ming the Merciless as a Roman general. Reprinted with permission of King Features Syndicate.

Figure 4. *Flash Gordon*: Ming with stereotypical Oriental features. Reprinted with permission of King Features Syndicate.

Figure 5. *Flash Gordon:*. Ming's headdress has a snake or dragon crest. Reprinted with permission of King Features Syndicate.

Figure 6. *Flash Gordon*: Dale Arden in 1930s fashion. Reprinted with permission of King Features Syndicate.

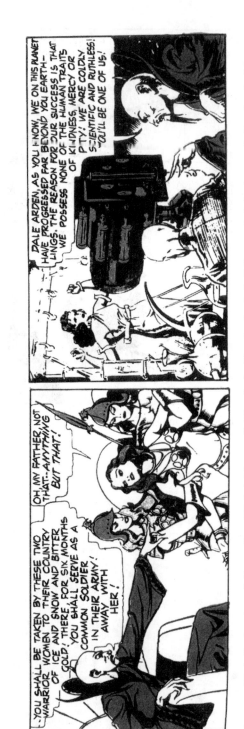

Figure 7. *Flash Gordon*: Aura (left panel) and Dale (right panel). They look alike, despite their different ethnic backgrounds. Reprinted with permission of King Features Syndicate.

Figure 8. *Terry and the Pirates:* Connie the Chinese servant with buckteeth, protruding ears, and beady eyes. Copyright Tribune Media Services, Inc. All rights reserved. Reprinted with permission.

Figure 9. Richard F. Outcault's *The Yellow Kid, New York World,* May 5, 1895.

Figure 10. *Terry and the Pirates*: Big Stoop, the loyal servant, and Terry, the young master. Copyright Tribune Media Services, Inc. All rights reserved. Reprinted with permission.

Figure 11. *Terry and the Pirates*: The Dragon Lady and her torture chamber. Copyright Tribune Media Services, Inc. All rights reserved. Reprinted with permission.

Figure 12. *Terry and the Pirates*: The Dragon Lady entertains Pat Ryan and Terry Lee. Copyright Tribune Media Services, Inc. All rights reserved. Reprinted with permission.

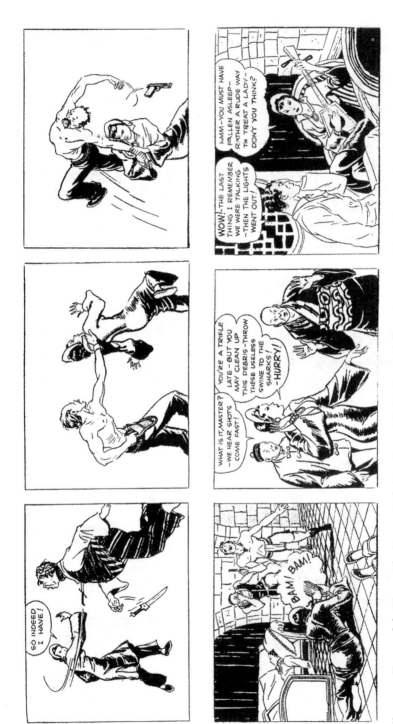

Figure 13. *Terry and the Pirates*: The Dragon Lady in action, while Pat Ryan is unconscious. Copyright Tribune Media Services, Inc. All rights reserved. Reprinted with permission.

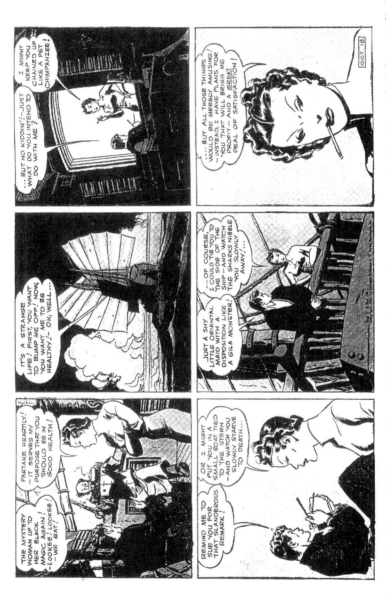

Figure 14. *Terry and the Pirates*: The Dragon Lady and Pat Ryan, two lovers trying to overpower each other. Copyright Tribune Media Services, Inc. All rights reserved. Reprinted with permission.

Figure 15. *Terry and the Pirates*: The Dragon Lady "conquered" or she stoops to conquer? Copyright Tribune Media Services, Inc. All rights reserved. Reprinted with permission.

Figure 16. *Terry and the Pirates*: Terry comforts the Dragon Lady, who shows more than maternal love. Copyright Tribune Media Services, Inc. All rights reserved. Reprinted with permission.

Figure 17. "Solid Sender" of *Terry and the Pirates*, rejected by the military newspapers. Copyright Milton Caniff 1943, 1945, 1959, 1982, 1987. Milton Caniff Estate permission — Harry Guyton, executor; Toni Mendez, Inc., representative.

Figure 18. *Male Call:* The inaugural strip changing Burma into Miss Lace. Copyright Milton Caniff 1943, 1945, 1959, 1982, 1987. Milton Caniff Estate permission — Harry Guyton, executor; Toni Mendez, Inc., representative.

Figure 19. *Male Call*: Miss Lace assists a soldier in writing a love letter. Copyright Milton Caniff 1943, 1945, 1959, 1982, 1987. Milton Caniff Estate permission — Harry Guyton, executor; Toni Mendez, Inc., representative.

Figure 20. *The Hands of Shang-chi, Master of Kung Fu*. Shang-chi Master of Kung Fu: TM & © 2000 Marvel Character, Inc. Used with permission.

Figure 21. *The Hands of Shang-chi, Master of Kung Fu.* Shang-chi Master of Kung Fu: TM & © 2000 Marvel Character, Inc. Used with permission.

CHAPTER TWO

Walt Disney's *Swiss Family Robinson*
Imperialist Ideology in Family Entertainment

Robinsonade

Harold Bloom once mused how *Robinson Crusoe* (1719) by a "politically incorrect Protestant imperialist" would fare in the "multicultural New Wave" (3). The fact that the imperialist archetype continues to be invoked, as in Bloom's collection of essays and, in popular culture, Walt Disney's *Swiss Family Robinson* (1960), the comic book *Space Family Robinson,* and William Hurt's *Lost in Space* (1998), demonstrates the appeal of "Robinsonade," stories of individuals struggling in hostile environments. Historically, Daniel Defoe's novel punctuated the emergence of Great Britain as a result of the alliance of England and Scotland, the Act of Union which Defoe vigorously publicized. In terms of literary history, Edward Said writes in *Culture and Imperialism* (1993) that *Robinson Crusoe* is the "prototypical modern realist novel," which, far from being an accident, deals with "a European who creates a fiefdom for himself" (xii). Beyond the British Isles, European culture proved to be equally fertile soil for Defoe's vision of imperialist expansion; therefore, a whole genre of "Robinsonade" featuring castaways on deserted islands took root on the Continent. The contribution to empire and masculinity building made by this adventure tale is incalculable, being *simultaneously* escapist and expansionist. Imperialist growth — its desire for, thrust into, occupation and often enslavement of alien cultures — is presented as *defensive measures,* as *strategies for survival.* Indeed, what better way is there to justify violence against other races than to locate the motive in self-preservation? Johann David Wyss's 1813 *The Swiss Family Robinson*

(*Der Schweizerische Robinson*) reworked the tradition in a significant way: he introduced a family rather than a single individual stranded on an island. On the eve of the golden age of imperialism, Wyss reinterpreted colonization not only as acts of personal heroism but as a family enterprise involving the joint effort of men, women, and children. Women and children (women are often viewed as children) played a key role in imperialism; moreover, they came to rationalize its existence. Wyss's story, therefore, was written for and about children and young adults, product and future progenitor of imperialist ideology. In 1960, the Disney Company adapted Wyss for a motion picture under the same title, directed by Ken Annakin, starring John Mills, Dorothy McGuire, and James MacArthur, long marketed as one of Disney's Family Film Collection of twelve videocassettes (figure 22). *Swiss Family Robinson* is available at video stores and supermarkets, and it is aired periodically on the Disney channel.

In the cultural history of Robinsonade, each text absorbs its predecessors and adds certain elements from its own conditions of production. While it is not my intention to detail the transfusions among Defoe, Wyss, and Disney, one similarity does stand out. To consolidate the nationalist, masculinist, and religious hegemony, all three texts pit antagonists against their heroes. These antagonists include the elements, human enemy without (aborigines or pirates), family members (contestants for the attention of the only eligible female on the island), and enemy within (heroes' own weaknesses). The last point surfaces most prominently in Defoe's text imbued with puritanism—Robinson Crusoe's original sin in not obeying his father's commands and not mending his ways as well as his later restoration by means of toiling on the island. The twenty-eight years on the island are replete with episodes that underline individuals' puniness, an experience that makes a devout Christian out of Crusoe. He spends years building a boat to take him to freedom, yet he never considers how to launch the boat, so it rots in the woods where it is built. When he does venture out to sea to survey another part of the island, the current takes him far away from land. Only through sheer luck does he return safely. Crusoe is also frightened by the aborigines' occasional ritual of cannibalism performed on the beach, an irony that seems to escape him. While he is stranded for almost three decades on this island, "savages" come and go as they please. While his body and mind are drained by loneliness, "savages" celebrate communally by shar-

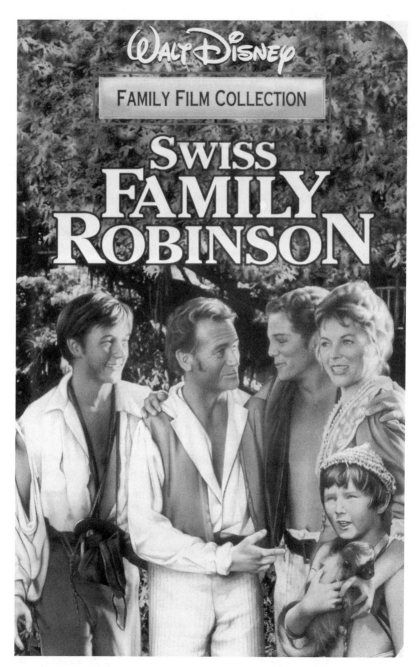

Figure 22. Disney's *Swiss Family Robinson* in videocassette.

ing human flesh. The subtlety of such events is beyond him; he simply turns to the Bible for consolation. This religious perspective is dramatically downplayed in the two subsequent texts. Wyss's island is more of a Garden of Eden and a tame colony than Defoe's. When it comes to Disney, characters merely pay lip service to God after arriving on the shore. The following pages concentrate on the first three types of antagonistic forces featured in Disney's film — nature, race (Oriental pirates), and gender (the Robinson boys' rivalry over a female).

Nature

The film opens, in medias res, with a ship besieged by howling winds and crushing waves, followed by the Robinson family — the parents, who remain unnamed and hence all the more symbolic, plus their three sons, Fritz, Ernst, and Francis — trapped in the ship's cabin, which is tilting to one side and fast filling with water. The family members' dialogue reveals that the ship comes to be in such a lurch because it was driven off course by pirates. This opening already establishes the animosity of nature and human, which brackets the film and which threatens the island paradise they are to occupy. The ensuing shipwreck also suggests the archetypal myth of Noah's ark, where human sins are cleansed and the survivors start afresh with residues of civilization bestowed by God — pairs of animals, muskets and gunpowder, books, clothings, a harpsichord, and an assortment of objects that the family had salvaged from the marooned vessel. Once the family members find themselves safely ashore, they say their prayers and immediately set out to explore the island. Discomfort with the alien surrounding is kept to a minimum, manifested exclusively through the mother figure. For instance, the first nights on the island are spent in a makeshift tent, culminating in a keen moment of distress seen in the parents' tête-à-tête, during which the Father repents of his grandiose dream of making it in the colony of New Guinea. Yet even this touch of remorse is alleviated by the thought that this island could be their New Guinea, now christened "New Switzerland." (In any case, the gloomy episode quickly dissolves in the scramble and childlike excitement as they seek shelter from the sudden tropical downpour.) The Mother is the only person of the family who has qualms over claiming the island as their home. Her concerns, expressions as much of timidity as of anything else, are practical and stereotypically maternal, one of which is the absence of girls for their boys on the island. Love and procreation become one of the doubts that mar this potential Eden. The Mother embodies the voice of thoughtfulness and prudence throughout the film; she serves as a check against the males' adventurous zeal. When the males enthusiastically escort her to the site of their future tree house, she is furious because the youngest son nearly falls from a tree limb. When the Mother is shown the completed tree house, her delight continues to be tinged with sadness. When the dilapidated ship is blown up for fear of giving away their whereabouts to the pirates, the Mother mumbles that she had dreamed of sailing home in it. When the opportunity arises at the end of the film for the family to return to Europe, all eyes focus on the Mother, for only she can give the final approval to stay and colonize.

Nevertheless, the family — including the Mother — claims the island de facto as its own. The family members' growing sense of proprietorship derives from the "civilized" order they impose on a bountiful Nature waiting to be exploited. A Darwinian arrogance manifests itself in the breathtaking speed with which they catalog and make use of things in this unknown territory. The encyclopedic exuberance serves as a scientific veneer to the Euro-American "civilizing mission," a modern rendition of the biblical edict to "be fruitful, and multiply, and replenish the earth, and subdue it" (Gen. 1:28). God's commands — "subdue it" and "multiply" — bespeak the human desire for exploitation of the external world. Despite inherent contradictions between science and Christianity, the twins inspire each other in the colonial project.

As such, the stunning array of animals that could not have possibly existed on the same island points to the oxymoron of scientific knowledge and wishful thinking, or wish fulfillment in the name of science. Wyss, consequently, allows penguins to wander on a tropical island of sugarcane and flamingos. A beached whale is made to provide much-needed blubber near a forest where kangaroos roam. In the same haphazard fashion, Disney features elephants, tigers, ostriches, zebras, and a host of other animals on an island situated close to Papua New Guinea. Although Disney spends less time than Wyss on the civilizing tasks of candle making, rubber producing, and pearl gathering, which give relatively few opportunities for cinematic action, the bizarre legion of animals constitutes some of the film's best comic skits.

Race

One comic skit appears to be harmless indeed but is, in fact, emblematic of the imperialist drive: the race of ostrich, dog, elephant, donkey, and zebra. This contest in the wilderness on the first national holiday of New Switzerland re-creates a semblance of civilization for the human "jockeys" and the spectators (the Mother, being a lady, sits on the sideline; the Father, future governor of the colony, officiates at first). The Robinsons simulate a civilized lifestyle by organizing the race, *play* as opposed to *work*, a leisured activity undertaken for no practical gains, supposedly after the civilizing mission has been largely completed. For play to achieve its purpose of relaxation, it must contain, paradoxically, an element of risk, or at least unpredictability. Because one's work is conducted in a routine, repetitive fashion for the upkeep or advancement of one's life, "games" come to enact human instincts normally suppressed during work, impulses such as yearnings for excitement and adventure. These emotions stem primarily from, as our modern society conceives it, competitions with fellow human beings.[1] Play can thus be regarded both as transcending base instincts of domination and as manifesting those very instincts. Indeed, *Swiss Family Robinson* is ambiguously positioned between these extremes. It records the morally reprehensible mind-set of imperialism, but it also reflects the human need for playfulness. Most viewers of *Swiss Family Robinson*, particularly children, will not bother to consider the larger context of this film. Instead, they will be taken in by its playfulness, resulting in an interpellation of imperialist ideology in the guise of family entertainment.

To illustrate, let us reread the "race" as a pun, denoting both a sports event and a biological-social subdivision of the human species. The race is fun not only because the outcome is uncertain but because another race of human beings poses danger by, literally, lurking in the horizon. After all, the prospect of winning is thwarted as much by the recalcitrant beasts they are riding and by contenders outstripping one another as by the intimations of deadly conflicts. During the race, the film intercuts to pirates surveilling the island, who are alerted to the presence of inhabitants by the firing of pistol to start the game. The least playful and apparently most peace-loving character, the Mother, in what could be construed as a subconscious wish for violence, pulls the trigger for the race of animals and for the final clash between races. (The behavior of Oriental pirates resembles that of animals.) Just as the exhilaration of a *race* is intensified by the possible confrontation with Oriental pirates, the popularity of the film as family entertainment relies on stereotypes of *race*.

Sessue Hayakawa and the Gang

Although both Wyss and Disney present their works as intended for children, they differ in one major respect. Disney is a throwback to the Defoe of the early eighteenth century in that the film revives Defoe's cannibalistic aborigines, utterly nonexistent in Wyss, through the presence of Oriental pirates marauding the waters. Whereas Wyss's characters have only Nature to contend with in establishing the colony New Switzerland, Disney includes human antagonists marked by racial difference from the family and from the majority of American moviegoers. The film does more than just add ferocious Asian pirates to the family's plights; Disney manipulates the motley band of cutthroats, who rattle sabers ceaselessly and utter animalistic cries, to bring forth the potential coup de grâce to the colonists' survival. In other words, the confidence of the Western man once enjoyed by Wyss living close to the golden age of imperialism is no longer available in the late 1950s and early 1960s. Wyss's island paradise, entirely at the disposal of the castaways and devoid of any aboriginal/human resistance, becomes a luxury for Disney. But heightened racial awareness does not deter the studio from making this film; instead, Disney turns Asians who are native to that part of the globe into savage intruders, ones to be repelled, if not exterminated, like the wicked half of Nature—storm to be endured, sharks to be shot at, tiger to be captured, python to be fended off.[2] By featuring buccaneer junks patrolling—in the words of Steve Frazee in his authorized edition of companion book for the film's release on December 10, 1960—"the uncharted islands in the Malay archipelago" (69), the motion picture almost laments the loss of Wyss's Eden, whose innocence is spoiled by the presence of Eden's own sons. The Western invaders are presented as rightful owners of the Earth.

Notwithstanding the fact that pirates occupy the peripheries of the protagonists' island world and thoughts, they are a recurring nightmare haunting the film in terms of the numerous, unexpected montages of the pirate junk and the Robinsons' verbal references to them. The Oriental other thus makes possible a tale of adventure and the identity of Western colonists. Serving no filmic purpose other than to silhouette the heroism of Caucasian protagonists, the pirate characters lack individuality; however, Disney takes great pains in costume, makeup (many white actors in yellowfaces and painted bodies), and dialogue (or the lack thereof) to assign a general Orientalist charateristic to the horde. As such, the buccaneers are all strangely clad and proffer myriad signs of Orientalness. Narratologically, these enemies without are pivotal: the junk emerges soon after the shipwreck to pose danger; the pirates' plunder rationalizes the entry into the family saga of Roberta, around whom the young men's romantic interests revolve; the impending attack by the buccaneers further justifies the memorable finale. Toward the end of the film, the family constructs lines of defense to protect the hilltop fortress. In the ensuing battle, the audience is treated to the spectacles of a collapsing bridge, a tiger pit, land mines, coconut bombs, stacks of logs tumbling down the steep hill, musket crossfires, and, eventually, hand-to-hand combat. Without the Asian horde, indeed, there would never have been the family entertainment billed in the Disney film.

Compared to the film, Frazee's book dwells at great length on the three pirate leaders: Kuala, AuBan, and Battoo. In particular, Kuala is in supreme command, portrayed as carrying a kris, the short Malay sword. In the Disney production, the archvillain Kuala played by Sessue Hayakawa seems to be the only member of the gang who is individualized. With his name occupying a brief moment in the opening credits and with his person most outlandishly attired (a cross between Japanese samurai and Malay warrior), Hayakawa presents the only recognizable face and name, the stereotypical images of his role notwithstanding. In the latter half of the film, Kuala dresses himself in the navy uniform taken from Roberta's grandfather, the captain of the ship plundered by pirates. Kuala's cross-dressing as a British captain mocks and threatens the maritime power so central to colonization of foreign lands. To reassert imperial control, Kuala is made to meet a tragic end.

Hayakawa joins this Disney project riding the tide of an Academy Award nomination for his performance as the Japanese prison camp commandant in *The Bridge on the River Kwai* (1957). Donald Kirihara, in "The Accepted Idea Displaced: Stereotype and Sessue Hayakawa," analyzes Hayakawa's career in the silent film era, specifically from 1914 to

1918. Kirihara argues that this actor, by the strength of "his distinctive performance style," aided externally by "the development of a classical narrational mode," succeeds in "ris[ing] above stock caricatures of the time" (81), a claim contradicted by Kirihara's own occasional statements and by at least one other contributor to the same collection of essays, *The Birth of Whiteness* (1996). Kirihara at one point acknowledges that "[t]he image of a thin veil of civility shrouding the menacing beast would remain part of Hayakawa's star personality throughout his career" (93). This seems an apt description of the archvillain Fu Manchu created by Sax Rohmer in the same period of the 1910s. Both Hayakawa's screen personae and Fu Manchu grow out of the paranoiac imagination of the "Yellow Peril." Nick Browne, in his essay on Madame Butterfly collected in *The Birth of Whiteness*, recognizes Kirihara's investigation of the "wide range of roles in the 1915–1918 period and after" for Hayakawa, but simultaneously reconfirms that "a number of significant films in the 1914–1915 period dramatically point to Hayakawa as a center of violence — murder or (fugitive) rape against white women" (229). Although not entirely sabotaging Kirihara's argument on the meteoric flash in Hayakawa's long career, Browne shortens it by one year. The point is not to quibble about the exact duration of Hayakawa's creative peak; rather, one must contextualize a series of performances, however brilliant, in that artist's corpus. Taken in the entirety of his work, Hayakawa's burst of energy, if indeed it is, in the 1910s seems the anomaly rather than the norm.

Furthermore, to accept Kirihara's assessment of Hayakawa's early career makes the actor's "fall" in 1960 so much lower by contrast and so much more excruciating to contemplate. Kuala in *Swiss Family Robinson* fits perfectly the stereotype of the malicious, barbaric, backstabbing Oriental, beyond the redemption of any clever critical maneuver. Hayakawa's performance as a fierce, bloodthirsty warlord displays few human emotions. While vocalizing unintelligible grunts and hollers throughout, Kuala does eventually speak a line or two of broken English. Meeting staunch resistance from the family's hilltop fortress, the chief pirate waves a white flag and orally communicates with the Father, while secretly ordering his men to mount the precipice from the rear for a surprise attack. The heavy accent and the pidgin English do give Kuala a voice, but only in such a way as to reinforce racist stereotypes of double-crossing Orientals, who converse in order to conquer. The flawed pidgin is itself fraught with racist connotations of imperfect, repugnant imitation of standard English. In Hayakawa's long career spanning half a century (he died in 1973), the short years in the 1910s are a rare moment for a talented, versatile Japanese American actor who is otherwise straitjacketed by racism in the film industry and in American culture.

Bertie/Roberta

There is yet another race in the latter half of the film. The two older Robinson boys, Fritz and Ernst, vie for the love of Roberta, the only eligible female on the island. Despite her youthful and beautiful appearance, Roberta plays a role similar to that of Asians. Imperialist ideology requires an aggressive masculinity bordering on a neurotic sexual energy, which is elicited from Fritz and Ernst as a result of the entry of Roberta into the story. Roberta, simply put, makes a man out of them, or rather, out of Fritz played by James MacArthur, whereas Ernst, rejected, leaves crestfallen. Roberta becomes a mirror onto which masculine desires project themselves, much in the way Asians are shrouded in the fears of the West as ancient as the "Yellow Peril" and as foreboding in 1960 as the mounting tension in Southeast Asia.

Roberta's choice of Fritz over Ernst goes beyond a mere matter of casting, what with James MacArthur's reputation, charming looks, and, especially, well-toned upper body (which is often exposed). By comparison, Ernst is lanky and adolescent. As the character Fritz describes himself, he is pragmatic, down-to-earth. Virile and resourceful in danger, he is bashful and awkward in the presence of Roberta—sort of a boyish, fledgling "quiet man" à la John Wayne. Ernst appears originally to lead in this sibling rivalry thanks to his sharp wit, flamboyance, and storage of massive information from reading. Ernst and Roberta also share a puerile fantasy for the refinement of high society. To appeal to her, Ernst even laboriously weaves a straw top hat, a symbol of culture they both yearn for. The hat is accidentally crushed during a fist fight with Fritz, who happens to be teaching Roberta how to shoot. Suspended between Ernst's fake culture and Fritz's reserved masculinity, Roberta seems to have made up her mind long ago, for she merely pretends to be a novice in the art of weaponry in order to physically get near Fritz. Her decision is somewhat preempted by character development; it seems natural that a product of the Magic Kingdom would have a desirable woman favor men over boys. No match for Fritz in their several clashes, Ernst behaves badly when his brother is caught in a python's coil, losing his compass and footing. On the contrary, MacArthur's youthful body is shown to contain great force, and the python succumbs after a prolonged battle. In a film perpetuating imperialist ideology, Roberta chooses manly qualities allegedly suitable for colonization in the wilderness. In a film designed for a young audience, Roberta invites hundreds of thousands of Ernsts to grow up into Fritzes. However, to suggest that the film only endorses Fritz's colonist image is not quite accurate. That Ernst alone returns to Europe at the closing strengthens rather than severs the family's bond with Western civilization. The island truly becomes New Switzerland, an outpost of the empire, a reincarnation of their home in Bern, Switzerland, because the Robinsons are even more closely connected with the Old World by means of the second son.

The transformation from boys to men is activated by the transformation from boy to girl-woman, or from Bertie to Roberta. The dual metamorphoses follow each other like chain reactions. To avoid humiliation at the hands of Sessue Hayakawa and the pirates after his ship is captured, Roberta's grandfather cuts her hair and cross-dresses her as Bertie the cabin boy. Unlike Hayakawa's British uniform, which threatens imperial stability, Roberta's cross-dressing reaffirms the gaps between genders and races, because a white female seeks protection from Orientals in the guise of a white boy. In the frantic escape from pirates, Roberta understandably does not stop to disclose her gender to her saviors, Fritz and Ernst, despite repeated hints at giving it away: she fails to keep up with the boys; she sits and shivers through the night rather than lying down with them. The truth is revealed when Fritz orders her to undress to cross the river. In the subsequent scuffle, Fritz realizes that she is a woman when he pins her to the ground. Mortified by their previous rudeness, Fritz and Ernst instantly take on the role of gentlemen eager to serve. Roberta, on the other hand, plays the part of a lady effortlessly. Setting out as a team to survey the island, Fritz and Ernst work well together, until a prize in Roberta presents itself and the brothers turn against each other, their facade of urbanity toward Roberta notwithstanding. The belligerence between Fritz and Ernst intensifies as Roberta dresses in their mother's apparel for the Christmas ball. Roberta's hair remains short but the dress of the film's only other female character, a traditional maternal figure, completely restores her gender. Both femininity and masculinity reside to an amazing degree in exterior accessories and demeanor that showcase certain opposite qualities.

Global Distribution and Me

"It was estimated," writes Douglas Gomery, "that one in three inhabitants of the planet had seen a Disney film" (74). Although the context in which Gomery's sentence appears suggests that he is commenting on the 1940s, one would like to think that he refers instead to the present. If Gomery's statement were indeed about a previous era, one would be aghast to ponder what the percentage of the world population would be who have been exposed to one form or another of Disney products since the end of World War II. This wide popularity has its roots in Walt Disney's bold strategies catering to baby boomers. The Disney television show premiered in 1954 and Disneyland in Anaheim, California, opened in 1955. The former was so successful that it was moved from Wednesday nights to Sunday nights in 1960 and remained on the air for more than two decades. The latter transformed modern society into an escapist theme park, with its clones in Florida, Japan, and France. A less profitable venture seems to be "live-action, adventure films aimed at family audiences, beginning with *20,000 Leagues Under the Sea* in 1955" (Gomery 75). *Swiss Family Robinson* finds itself in the company of such Disney family films as *Old Yeller* (1957), *The Shaggy Dog* (1959), *Toby Tyler* (1960), *The Absent-minded Professor* (1961), *Son of Flubber* (1962), *The Misadventures of Merlin Jones* (1964), and *That Darn Cat* (1965).

Granted that some of the other family films are more American-oriented, *Swiss Family Robinson* has a distinctly Anglo-American and European flavor. This characteristic arises from the characters' accents. In addition to the gobbled-up pidgin English and presumably native languages used by Sessue Hayakawa, the Euro-American characters have two different accents. The Father and the Mother, joined by Roberta and her grandfather, speak British English, whereas the three Robinson boys speak American English. The young Robinsons' accent helps the target audience — American teenagers — identify with the adventure, while the older Robinsons' accent provides nostalgic linkages to European imperialism. Switzerland, however, had not been particularly known for its imperial history, which perhaps prompted Wyss's nationalist project. Disney adroitly deflects Wyss's nationalism, rendering "Swiss" and "Robin-son" in the title mere signifiers for *every* family.

In the era of global cinema, family films such as *Swiss Family Robinson* will most likely not become dated, as it could be widely disseminated on videocassette, DVD, or laser disc. Imperialist ideology is perpetu-ated not only through the content of the film but through the capital-ist, neo-imperialist circulation of the film. The market of "a global cin-ema audience of two hundred million people" (Buck 122) is too large for Disney's Family Film Collection to ignore. The global audience, includ-ing Asians maligned in the film, does not seem particularly troubled by the intersection of family entertainment and imperialist ideology. Asian viewers would probably join in the family's hurrays when retreating pi-rates disintegrate into canon fodder. The colonization of the mind out-lives the postwar decolonization movement in the Third World, thanks in part to seemingly wholesome family fun Walt Disney offers. I can testify to this subtle cultural imperialism firsthand. It was probably my dad who took me to see *Swiss Family Robinson* at a movie theater in Taipei, Taiwan, in what must have been a rare family outing during the economically austere, if not depressed, early 1960s. Two fragmented yet vivid images stayed with me and assured me that this particular film was the one I had seen in my childhood: the awesome tree house and, alas, the cheers, including my own, over the logs' crushing of scoundrels who looked most like me. Three decades later, as I first reviewed the film for the present project, my then two-and-half-year-old daughter kept repeating in Mandarin "*Huai-ren! Huai-ren!*" ("Bad Guys!" "Bad Guys!") whenever pirates graced the TV screen.[3]

Part II
Clash of Arms

CHAPTER THREE

Martial Metaphors and Asian America

Martial Artists

In the 1960s and 1970s, a new image of the East arose out of the tumultuous U.S. domestic and international conditions: the civil rights movement, the hippie counterculture, demonstrations, and countless assassinations, on the one hand; the escalating Vietnam War, the gradual shift of the world's economic center to the Pacific Rim (including "the four little dragons"), the attendant need for entertainment and the surge of the Asian film industry, and the opening of China in the wake of President Nixon's 1972 visit, on the other. Within such a volatile milieu, something in an ordinary martial arts practitioner, Bruce Lee, clicked with the times, catapulting him to international fame. Lee came to symbolize the spirit of combativeness, simultaneously appealing to the Asian, Asian American, American, and perhaps world audience. These various groups of viewers read in Lee expressions of their own desires and anxieties. Lee, simply put, crystallized the phenomenon of the martialization of cultures, cultures in conflict with one another or with themselves.

Although kung fu has always been part of the Asian tradition, the current martialization of America seems so widespread that it does not require much astuteness to discern. In any medium-sized town across the United States, it is almost certain that one could find at least one martial arts school (*do-kuan* or *dojo*) for adults and children. The clientele for these schools are principally Americans rather than Asians. Martial arts has been Americanized and internationalized, now a part of human activities. Beyond the physical existence of such *do-kuan,* U.S.

popular culture is permeated with martial arts images. Should proof of its popularity be needed, films and TV provide ample evidence. As quintessentially American as Disney has become, one of its full-length animations, *The Lion King* (1994), features a wise baboon, Rafiki,[1] as a strange mixture of African wise man, Zen master, and Bruce Lee. Rafiki leads the wayward Simba back to the spirit of his father, the Lion King, and to his duty as the heir apparent among the lion pride by means of a series of mystical, paradoxical Zen sayings and behavior ("*koan*"). The baboon hits Simba on the head with his walking staff in a way a Zen master frequently adopts to shock and awaken the disciple. The baboon even presents himself in a cross-legged posture, with palms facing upward and resting on his knees, clearly an imitation of transcendental meditation. The baboon eventually assists Simba in defeating his wicked uncle, Scar, and the pack of hyenas. The baboon does this with much fanfare based on kung fu poses, emitting the strident, high-pitched fighting yells that have evolved into one of Bruce Lee's trademarks. More recently, George Clooney's Batman character in *Batman and Robin* (1997) presents combat tableaux closely resembling martial arts forms. Clooney does not produce more of kung fu maneuvers probably because, unlike animations, the actor must be able to do some on his own.

In view of the proliferating martial metaphors in popular culture, why is there such scant academic attention? Few systematic studies have been engaged thus far to analyze kung fu films; most book-length writings on this topic are popular, journalistic reports, evidenced in Alex Ben Block's *The Legend of Bruce Lee* (1974) and Marilyn D. Mintz's *The Martial Arts Films* (1978). Ironically, some academically trained scholars have embarked on a career related to the East as a result of exposure to kung fu. In the preface to *Romance and the "Yellow Peril": Race, Sex, and Discursive Strategies in Hollywood Fiction* (1993), Gina Marchetti confesses that a woman with an Italian surname writing a book on Asians in motion pictures seems odd. Her interest in Asian cultures, she explains, began quite accidentally in 1982 when she went to a kung fu class with her friend. She continued to train and watch kung fu films some ten years later. Marchetti's honest admission notwithstanding, most scholars may secretly feel that kung fu films are beneath them, which surfaces as well in my own ambiguous reaction to Bruce Lee: my adolescent fetishization of Bruce Lee juxtaposed with my present embarrassment over earlier fetishization.

Indeed, it is very tough to sit through Bruce Lee's films twenty some years after I first viewed them as a teenager in Taiwan. The films have a slipshod quality—plot, set, acting, cinematography, editing, dialogue, and sound track—compounded by Lee's mediocre, at times incredibly poor, acting, which periodically erupts into well-choreographed, though near-hysterical, battle scenes. Having lived in the West for some time now, I find those moments of martial arts particularly unsettling because they fall into the stereotype of the barbaric Oriental. Although none of the films depict him in the image of the archvillain Fu Manchu, Lee's ruthless superhuman energy lends itself to such a coupling with evil. In fact, a familial relationship is established between Fu Manchu and a Shang-chi, modeled on Bruce Lee, as the opening sequence of Marvel Comics' 1973 *The Hands of Shang-chi, Master of Kung Fu* makes clear (figures 20 and 21). Against the background of a Fu Manchu with goatees, slant eyes, and claws with sharp nails, Shang-chi is presented as "born to be the world's most fearsome fighter, yet also born to carry the cruellest curse in mankind's memory—because his father is the most infamous villain of all time—FU MANCHU." Full of stale hyperboles, this comic strip intensifies the fetish of Bruce Lee by coalescing him with the archetype of the Yellow Peril, as indeed the comics proceed to do in gradually fading a series of panels from Shang-chi into Fu Manchu.

None of the fighting scenes in Lee's films are so long as to be boring, which cannot be said about the rest of Lee's lackluster performance— mere frames to justify the explosion of violence. Lee's contorted facial and body muscles in action are at once the revolting and the mesmerizing focal point for the spectacle of blood and gore. Although abhorring the amount of violence in his films, I tend to agree with Stuart Kaminsky's observation that Bruce Lee's "ballet of violence" (*American Film Genres* 77) takes after Fred Astaire's or Gene Kelly's musicals. Dana Polan, in "Brief Encounters: Mass Culture and the Evacuation of Sense," believes that Kaminsky goes on to give a sociological interpretation of the films. Polan maintains that Kaminsky sees the rituals of violence in Hong Kong kung fu films as symbolic of the masses, embodied in the lower-class hero, rebelling against patriarchal culture, crystallized in the evil father figure. In contrast to Kaminsky, Polan cites Claudine Eizykman's *La jouissance-cinéma* (1976). Eizykman, an avant-garde, deconstructionist filmmaker, contends that kung fu battles are "pure visual and aural spectacle . . . a display of movements and sounds that ceases to be about anything but its own kinesis" (Polan 168). Whereas Eizykman chooses to read violence as devoid of social context and consequences, Kaminsky's sociological approach similarly grows out of a fascination with kung fu's physical movements. Yet this shared view of the aesthetics of violence results in much controversy.

Critics have long alleged that such representations of violence lead to antisocial behavior because they advocate violence as the solution to problems. Even a piece as neutral as Kaminsky's "Kung Fu Film as Ghetto Myth," in which he describes the idolization of Bruce Lee among urban blacks, could conceivably be used to support critics' contention that martial arts fuels inner-city violence. At the other end of this spectrum of views, Rene Girard's theory of scapegoating locates ritualistic sacrifice of innocent victims at the heart of any culture. By examining the Bible, Greek mythology, medieval and even modern "persecution texts," documents written by nonconscious persecutors, Girard advances the daring thesis that violence and the sacred are inseparable. Modern life, however, is largely stripped of ancient myths and religious zeal. The human need for projecting fear and anxiety onto characters such as Satan and Jews remains, nevertheless, as urgent as ever. Moviegoing or video viewing in a fantasy world, with the attendant sense of separation from reality, constitutes a collective rite whereby the audience exteriorizes its phobia and aggression onto the antagonists on the screen, antagonists marked by, consistent with Girard's generalizations, foreignness and physical handicap. Girard's hypothesis seems to be borne out by the evil characters in *Enter the Dragon* (1973) — Han with a fake arm equipped with animal claws of various sizes, aided by his Western henchman with a deep facial scar. Films and TV become modern rites of collective cleansing of psychosis.

To study Bruce Lee's corpus in such a light sharpens entangled issues of race, colonialism, and audience reception. Lee's brash and masculine image is undoubtedly the key to his stardom. But more important, Lee succeeds in the world market because his films contain levels of ambivalence, allowing different segments of primarily male population to identify with Lee. His films are anticolonialist and colonialist at once. To the Chinese audience, Bruce Lee, whose first name means "Little Dragon," stands as a nationalist hero. Not only do his films invoke, in a heavy-handed and campy way, the beloved, mythical symbol of China — the dragon — but Lee's characters are often associated with the dragon. The protagonist in *Return of the Dragon* (also translated as *The Way of the Dragon* [1972]) is called Tang Lung ("China Dragon"). Equally patriotic, the protagonist in *The Chinese Connection* (1972) smashes the plague of "Sick Man of East Asia," a derogatory name for China given by the Japanese around the turn of the twentieth century. A reflection of the historical animosity the Chinese harbor against Japan, the Japanese are invariably demonized, the Japanese martial arts — karate and judo — ridiculed. Lee combats other foreign opponents as well. Filmed in Thailand, *Fists of Fury* (1971) presents many Southeast Asian thugs. *The Chinese Connection,* set in Shanghai in 1908, introduces Japanese imperialists and their Russian mercenary. In the final duel of *Return of the Dragon,* Lee slays Chuck Norris at the Roman coliseum (figure 23). Lee in *Enter the Dragon,* which unfolds in modern-day Hong Kong, kills a Western martial arts expert, among others. In the posthumously completed and released *Game of Death* (1977), the only footage filmed prior to his death in 1973 features Bruce Lee terminating Western fighters, including Kareem Abdul-Jabbar.

On the other hand, granted that the West is portrayed as imperialistic and decadent, the colonial mentality of Hong Kong and of many Chi-

Figure 23. Bruce Lee and Chuck Norris in *Return of the Dragon.* Courtesy of Photofest.

nese moviegoers renders the West as an object of desire, with his films often set in exotic foreign countries. While the sense of colonial oppression felt by the audience is somewhat alleviated by Lee's prowess, the colonized nevertheless relish the tour of Rome in *Return of the Dragon*, written and directed by Lee himself. The ultimate irony lies in Bruce Lee himself. His fame in the Chinese-speaking world derives in large measure from his anti-West, anti-Japan filmic personae, which are silhouetted against years of apprenticeship in Hollywood. The nationalist appeal of Lee's roles is predicated on the defeat of Western antagonists, who are all real-life friends and disciples of Bruce Lee's.

To the Western audience, the Chinese hero confronts his enemies with an amazing amount of savagery, one that befits the stereotype of "Yellow Peril" in the Western consciousness. Just as an audience cheers the hero's triumph, which echoes the worldwide decolonization in the late 1960s, one could secretly retain the age-old bias against the Orient. *Enter the Dragon*, in addition, offers touristic voyeurism of the exotic boat people in the Hong Kong harbor. The episode on the American fighters' arrival amid a fleet of junks is shot from the perspective of foreign gazes. The colonial psyche being what it is, Lee's films ceaselessly shuttle between a domestic, Chinese viewpoint and the Western one. To make possible the double vision, Lee's filmic personae frequently befriend both white and black Americans. The African American character played by Jim Kelly in *Enter the Dragon* even displays social consciousness of the time: he is harassed by white policemen and comments on the similarity of life of the downtrodden, whether in U.S. ghettos or among Hong Kong boat people. The African American is ultimately expendable, and is tortured to death, thus leaving his white Vietnam War comrade, another martial artist, to assist Lee in the final contest against Han.

A posthumously completed film such as *Game of Death* is bound to be perplexing. The audience knows well that the virile Bruce Lee, not long after shooting the prolonged fighting finale, died in the bed of the Taiwanese actress Betty Ting Pei. Allegedly at Ting Pei's apartment to discuss the script, Lee was said to be afflicted with headache so severely that he took a prescription painkiller, Equagesic, and sought the comfort of Ting Pei's bed. According to Alex Ben Block, Lee had earlier passed out a number of times on the set and had subsequently been diagnosed as suffering from epilepsy. The autopsy revealed that traces of cannabis or marijuana were left in his stomach and his brain was swollen, a symptom of edema. When I queried Linda Lee Cadwell, Bruce Lee's widow, on Block's assertion of an epileptic Lee during her book promotion tour for the first three volumes of what was projected to be the twelve-volume Bruce Lee Library, she responded that Lee did faint in the studio, but later physical tests in the United States revealed that Lee had "the body of an eighteen-year-old" and that "the seizures were of no known causes."[2] Note that despite an immediate, unequivocal repudiation of Block's claim, she opted for a word — "seizures" — suspended between the harmless "fainting" and the potentially devastating "epilepsy." "Seizures" usually mean muscular convulsions as a result of neurological short-circuits. Thus, the paragon of strength and masculinity turned out to have been afflicted with mysterious seizures, moments when one was utterly out of control.

With only limited footage shot before Lee's death in 1973, the "unique," "unrivaled" Bruce Lee appears merely in the closing moments of the duels with four martial artists — two Asians and two Westerners. Elsewhere in the film, awkward devices are resorted to in an effort to veil the substitute's face: wide-rimmed sunglasses, shots from the back, dim lighting, disfigured face due to a gunshot wound and plastic surgery, motorcycle helmet, and so forth. It is ironic that while kung fu films thrive on the publicity of actors/actresses performing their own daredevil stunts, this film uses the look-alike throughout. Stuart Kaminsky, among others, has pointed out that the genre of martial arts films promotes itself on "total performance [of martial artists] . . . without cutting away to other angles or close ups [sic]. In a Bazinian sense, our acceptance of the myth is based to a great degree upon our belief that the performer is actually doing these things" (*American Film Genres* 74). This emphasis on the authenticity and the credibility of the performance stems from the Chinese opera and theater tradition, where performers from an early age undergo rigorous training to be, at once, singers, dancers, acrobats, makeup artists, and whatnot. Bruce Lee's father was an opera singer; Bruce Lee's heir apparent in today's Hong Kong cinema, Jackie Chan, was trained to be an opera singer.

Bruce Lee himself was apprenticed not just in the martial arts tradition of China but in Hollywood, an unparalleled credential at the time which helped launch his career. Bruce Lee played the Japanese houseboy and chauffeur Kato in the twenty-six episodes of the TV series *The Green Hornet* during the 1966–67 season. Lee also appeared in the film *Marlowe*

(1969), and four episodes of the 1970 TV series *Longstreet*. In these minor
roles, Lee invariably played the kung fu master, punching, kicking, and
issuing what later developed into his distinctive "cat-like kiai, or fighting yell" (Block 80). However, when Bruce Lee's big chance came along
in the television series *Kung Fu* (aired from 1972 to 1975), the lead role
of Kwai Chen Caine was lost to David Carradine. Carradine was perhaps
a better actor than Lee, but Lee was definitely a better martial artist than
Carradine. The decision over casting was based not so much on performance techniques as on audience reception. In fact, the series went to great
lengths to justify a Caucasian-looking protagonist: the Hollywood cliché
of a mixed-blood was recycled to account for an American-looking boy
training at the Shaolin Temple and, later, a Carradine wandering among
Chinese communities across the American West. Passing over a true Eurasian such as Bruce Lee (whose grandmother is British), the series has a
Caucasian with taped eyes passing for a Eurasian. The choice of Carradine manifests the entrenched Orientalism that entails an easier audience
identification with the protagonist who is Caucasian. Yet this Orientalist
perception infiltrates cultures and human relationships so thoroughly
that even Asian viewers succumb to it, evidenced by masses of Asian
fans for Bruce Lee in the 1970s and for Jackie Chan in the 1990s, oblivious to the coexistence of Chinese pride and Chinese subservience in
their films.

Comparing the TV pilot of *Kung Fu* with the subsequent series, David
Carradine in the pilot appears to be much more *natural*: he speaks normally, with slight affectation in accent, unlike the later protagonist who
spews forth fortune-cookie aphorisms in a halting, pidginized mono-
tone; his movements are more spontaneous, with less of the later protagonist's low bows and blank, childlike look. Caine in the pilot has short-
cropped hair, recently grown from a monk's shaved head. In the series,
his hair becomes the fashionable 1970s long hair. The series both Orientalized and hippie-ized Caine in keeping with the growing ethos of the
time. With *Kung Fu* an expression of the Orientalist cult, the titles to
many of its episodes reveal the 1970s yearning for spirituality: "Dream
within a Dream"; "The Demon's Champion"; and "The Demon God,"
the last directed by Carradine himself. These episodes posit that the true
enemy lies within, symptomatic of the withdrawal into the self after the
failure of the 1960s utopian vision for a radically altered society. The
cultural alternative proposed by the series glaringly contradicts the pilot's

activist closure. At the end of the TV pilot, a militant Caine, after killing the Shaolin bounty hunter, sets fire to the railroad that epitomizes the exploitation of fellow Chinese coolies. Such militancy is toned down considerably in subsequent episodes. The pilot in 1972 reflects the stridency of the civil rights movement and antiwar sentiment, whereas its successors retreat to mystical esotericism, heralding the New Age movement so vibrant at the threshold of the twenty-first century.

Another consistent motif linking the pilot and the series is the flashbacks, which demonstrate the derivativeness of the series. The series' flashbacks to the pilot show are instrumental in telling Caine's past, the story of how an interracial child becomes an apprentice at the Shaolin Temple. Key moments in Caine's memory of his training at the temple and his devotion to his masters, these flashbacks are endlessly rehashed in the series. The temple scenes are products of Orientalist kitsch, with puzzling Chinese sayings and embarrassing kung fu matches, all melodramatically staged among rows of candles, all arrested in blurred frames and fading shots.

It would be wrong to dismiss *Kung Fu* as merely Western filmmakers, crew, and actors regurgitating Orientalist images for the Western viewers. Orientalism has interpellated the Asian and Asian American mind as well. The production of such films requires the collaboration of Asians and Asian Americans. The cast for each episode almost always includes Asian Americans. Behind the scenes, the concluding credits to *Kung Fu* reveal that the technical or kung fu adviser, who is responsible for orchestrating the main allure of the series, is always someone with an Asian-sounding name. Even Jackie Chan, heir apparent to Bruce Lee in Hong Kong's kung fu films, continues the paradox of attraction and repulsion vis-à-vis the West. Chan, however, defines himself in contradistinction to Lee's image. Whereas Lee's fighting is marked by fury, Chan plays the clown in the style of traditional Chinese operas.[3] Whereas Lee smashes his opponent's skull, Chan, in a manner of speaking, scratches and tickles him. Of course, Lee at times tries to perform a skit or two, but never with the kind of success that the born comedian Chan achieves. For instance, Lee pretends to be an electrician with a silly grin in *The Chinese Connection*; he plays the country bumpkin in *Fists of Fury* and in *Return of the Dragon*. Likewise, the turning point in the duel in *Return of the Dragon* arrives when Lee, in slapstick fashion, plucks the body hair on Chuck Norris's chest.

Jackie Chan has built his career by transforming the kung fu fad of an earlier decade inaugurated by Bruce Lee. As the closing credits roll in Jackie Chan's *Supercop* (1996), the film follows a Chan tradition of showing "outtakes," footage that failed to make it into the film, a customary method to impress upon the audience Chan's "total performance" without the use of stuntmen. Chan *is* the stuntman, which is the crux of his reputation. These fragments of "rejects" contain both comic moments such as Chan forgetting his line and, above all, hair-raising moments of Chan's well-publicized accidents. In *Supercop,* this occurs when Chan, hanging in mid-air, is hit by the prop of an oncoming helicopter. As for the leading actress, Michelle Khan,[4] she manages, after several trials and errors, to land her motorcycle on top of a moving train. But the sound track to this closing footage is Tom Jones redoing the 1970s Carl Douglas hit "Kung Fu Fighting." The slightly revised song in Tom Jones's still sonorous voice interweaves a multitude of richly nostalgic and intertextual strands, all founded on a similar myth: a 1970s African American singer supposedly reflecting the longing of the disenfranchised black community; an erstwhile internationally renowned singer allegedly out of the coal mines in Wales; a short-lived kung fu legend who made it by embodying the turmoil of the times; a Shaolin monk, wanted by the Ching dynasty, turned a fugitive in the American West; a Jackie Chan who rose from a much-abused Chinese opera apprentice to a sensation in Asia, poised now to capture the global cinema market. Chan accomplishes this through performing ever more difficult stunts, inflicting on himself numerous bodily injuries, which all receive extensive media coverage. One can only wonder about this self-punishing, high-risk lifestyle of a billionaire actor already in his forties. This reluctance to let go of the limelight surely stems less from financial than from psychological needs — perhaps the longing for attention and accolade as a result of traumatized early experience. At any rate, the myth of triumph in spite of adversity is inherent in the kung fu genre, subject to borrowing by any individual or any group identifying with the besieged hero.[5] Such is the motivation for the deployment of martial metaphors in Asian American writing emerging in the 1970s and thriving in later decades.

Artists

For marginalized Asian American writers to empower themselves in the 1970s, two martial metaphors from the Asian heritage came to their aid:

the god of war and art Guan Gung (variously transliterated as Gwan Gung or Gwan Goong) and the woman warrior Fa Mu Lan. Although both are legendary figures in China and initially resorted to almost exclusively in Chinese American texts, no one can deny that their images intertwine with every facet of the contemporary Asian American cultural production. Not that Chinese Americans stand for Asian Americans in an ethnocentric way, but warrior icons borrowed from Chinese history have come to symbolize the ethnic struggle of a community, one imagined and conceived in the 1960s to gain political leverage.

That male Asian American writers find inspiration in Guan Gung while their female counterparts do so in Fa Mu Lan demonstrates the different needs of each gender. The "godfather" of Asian American plays, Frank Chin, employs the male deity, whose stylized image often appears absorbed in a volume of book, with his gigantic green-dragon crescent-shaped knife resting on his side. Chin's reliance on Guan Gung is ubiquitous, both in his plays and in the prefaces to his coedited *Aiiieeeee!* (1974) and *The Big Aiiieeeee!* (1991). In addition to Guan Gung, the playwright draws his strength from other supposedly masculinist activities as well, such as boxing in *The Chickencoop Chinaman* (premiered in 1972). David Henry Hwang likewise evokes Guan Gung in *The Dance and the Railroad*. Hwang's two characters, on strike against the exploitative continental railroad company, practice opera moves for a performance in honor of Guan Gung. On the other hand, female Asian American writers model their strong women characters on goddesses. The narrator in Amy Tan's *The Kitchen God's Wife* reverses the tradition of the Kitchen God to venerate his spouse. There is no reason why divinities of the opposite sex cannot coexist in the same work. Genny Lim, in the concluding moments of the film *Paper Angels* (1982), allows two detainees on Angel Island in 1915 to pray to deities of their own choosing. Fong burns incense to and entreats the statuette of Guan Gung, whereas Ku Ling imagines herself becoming the heroine "Fei Shan" beheading barbarians. The fact that male and female characters seek solace from deities of their own sex may be less important than their shared fate of imprisonment and humiliation, which calls for self-empowerment. Anxiously appealing to reverse the denial of entry, Fong has been stranded on the island the longest among fellow inmates, so long, in fact, that the play portrays him as a homosexual stripped of his masculinity. Despite her vehement protest, Ku Ling is baptized and christened as the biblical "Ruth" by Miss Gregory, the self-righteous missionary, to denote her conversion to a new Christian, Western identity.

A more recent and direct artistic connection with martial artists is Peter Bacho's short autobiographical story "The Second Room," collected in his *Dark Blue Suit and Other Stories* (1997). Recording his late-1960s experience of training at the Seattle martial arts school established by Bruce Lee, Bacho practiced in the absence of Lee, who had left for Hollywood at the time. Bacho's fascination with kung fu derived from his inner-city and Filipino background, where young adults proved their virility by enduring physical hardships and abuses on the basketball court, in the boxing ring, and in other arenas of potential violence. The identical rules of the game applied at the Bruce Lee school, where a separate "second" room for one-on-one combat allowed for what amounted to merciless street fighting. During his matches with the infamous Killer in the second room, Bacho was saved only through the interventions of Taky and Roy, Lee's students who ran the place. It stands to reason that the practice of the second room was a legacy of Bruce Lee, faithfully preserved by his disciples during the days Bacho attended the classes.

None was as instrumental in martializing the Asian American cultural expression in the 1970s as Maxine Hong Kingston. Yet in view of the machismo characteristic of kung fu, amply demonstrated by Bacho's fond memories of the second room, no wonder a feminist writer such as Kingston would remain ambivalent and deconstructive with regard to martial tropes, while seeking self-empowerment through them. Martial metaphors, with their spirit of contestation and their Asian origin, simply befit the Asian American struggle for identity. The titles of Kingston's works are steeped in the Chinese martial arts tradition: *The Woman Warrior* (1976) fantasizes the career of a "female avenger"; the derogatory racial epithet that is the title of *China Men* (1980) calls for resistance; *Tripmaster Monkey* (1989) borrows the resourceful trickster-rebel, the Monkey King, from the sixteenth-century Chinese classic *Journey to the West*.

Indeed, the fire of the warring 1960s and 1970s has never been extinguished at the heart of each of Kingston's books. But just as the three books move farther away from the turbulent decade in terms of publication dates, they somehow become more squarely set in the 1970s. As I discussed in my book, *Immigrant Subjectivities in Asian American and Asian Diaspora Literatures* (1998), *The Woman Warrior* enjoys a tremendous following not only because it reflects the tumultuous 1970s, but because it kneads together a mythical Orient with feminist yearnings. It is important to note that *The Woman Warrior* is located more in an exotic, imaginary land than in the streets of the United States. Although retaining the parable quality of its predecessor in the shorter pieces, such as "On Discovery" on Tang Ao, *China Men* is relatively muted and realistic. With its heavy documentation of the sufferings of early Chinese immigrants, *China Men* is largely devoid, to use Sau-ling Cynthia Wong's term, of the "extravagance" of imagination in *The Woman Warrior*. Critics and the public, as a result, find this sequel pale in comparison. When the long-awaited *Tripmaster Monkey* comes along in 1989, the novel returns resolutely to the 1970s, its fragmentary style and its near-schizophrenic protagonist embodying the decade's agitation and confusion. Ironically, this novel anchored so closely to the heart of confrontations of the time, namely, in San Francisco, is deemed the least relevant to the decade, evidenced by critical indifference to it. This may be caused ultimately by Kingston's diametrically opposed treatments of struggle in the first and the third books. Despite its otherworldly flights of fancy, *The Woman Warrior* launches assault with a vengeance against its multiple enemies: the Vietnam War, war over race, and war over gender. On the other hand, in *Tripmaster* war becomes increasingly a wordplay. It is small wonder, then, that the general audience takes the first book seriously and the third lightly.

To be fair to Kingston, however, her antiwar, pacifist stance with regard to the Vietnam War has never wavered. Throughout her books, the rhetoric linking industries, businesses, and governments with the war machine persists. One of the essays, "War," collected in *Hawaii One Summer* (1987), states that Kingston, her husband, and their son left the mainland in 1967 for Hawaii "in despair over the war." Kingston goes on to write: "It was the duty of the pacifist in a war economy not to work" (13), leading the Kingstons to live as scavengers for some time. Just as the concern over Vietnam is concentrated in one story of *Hawaii One Summer,* which as a whole depicts the magical beauty of the tropical paradise, the Vietnam War accounts for a small part of the martial metaphors in Kingston as well.

In *China Men*, the chapter titled "The Brother in Vietnam" deals specifically with the Vietnam War, or rather, the preparation not to go to the war. The protagonist, the narrator's brother, teaches young students from disadvantaged backgrounds purportedly with low IQs. The war only occurs in the brother's nightmares. Correctly identifying "an antiwar motif" in the book, and specifically in "The Brother in Vietnam," King-Kok Cheung nonetheless considers this motif tangential to her argument, as she expends only half a page, or one paragraph, on it (*Articulate Silences* 119). But martial metaphors proliferate in Kingston. The Chinese immigrants' lives in *China Men*, it goes without saying, are records of their defeats and intermittent triumphs.

Although it was published in 1989, *Tripmaster Monkey* takes place in the 1970s in San Francisco, filled with the decade's rocking, rollicking, fluctuating, shifting language and consciousness. The protagonist, Wittman Ah Sing, appears always on edge, so sensitive that he strikes one as hysterical, even schizophrenic. Ceaselessly spewing forth words in a high-speed monologue and interior monologue, Wittman is in dire need of his namesake, the Monkey King, whose magic of seventy-two transformations serves, at least in Wittman's mind, to buttress him in his search for identity.

The novel opens with an FOB (Fresh-Off-the-Boat) immigrant seen as doing the kind of walk in "kung fu movies when they are full of contentment on a sunny day" (5). Wittman subsequently comments with some anger on *The Lady from Shanghai* with Orson Welles and Rita Hayworth: " 'Oriental.' Shit." But the whole passage on the FOB's body and pidgin derives from Orientalism.[6] In the chapter titled "A Pear Garden in the West" toward the end of *Tripmaster Monkey*, Wittman orchestrates a read-through of his play. The Pear Garden is the site where the three warriors Liu Pei, Guan Gung, and Chan Fei in the fourteenth-century classic *The Romance of the Three Kingdoms* vow to be brothers and "die on the same day" in battle. This read-through involves key symbols of the martial heritage. After a cameo appearance by Siew Loong (Bruce Lee's Chinese name), the script rolls on to *The Romance of the Three Kingdoms* and *Journey to the West* about the Monkey King.

To return to Kingston's magnum opus, *The Woman Warrior* touches on the conflict in Indochina only through occasional references to the narrator Maxine's brother serving in Vietnam. Pushed to the foreground, instead, is traditional martial arts popularized by Hong Kong films of chivalrous swordsmen (*wu-hsia-pien*). Compared to Bruce Lee, films of chivalrous swordsmen are set in the more distant past and utilize swords rather than fists. The centerpiece of the martial imagery, the chapter titled "White Tigers," models itself on the trite formula of the kung fu genre:

apprenticeship, followed by duel or tournament. But Kingston explicitly describes her approach in "White Tigers" as parodic: she treats the chapter not as "a Chinese myth but one transformed by America, a sort of kung fu movie *parody*" ("Cultural Mis-readings" 57; emphasis in the original). Dangling between modernist irony and postmodernist pastiche,[7] Kingston demonstrates a condescending attitude whenever deploying kung fu symbols from American and Asian popular cultures. At the most blatant, Kingston lashes out saying that "martial arts are for unsure little boys kicking away under fluorescent lights" (*The Woman Warrior* 62). Even as the novelist painstakingly and lovingly molds the career of the woman warrior, the tone of high seriousness in the first half of "White Tigers" is at times debunked by abrupt American points of reference. Immediately after the novice politely declines food, the reader encounters in a parenthesis, as if hearing Maxine's aside, that she "like[s] chocolate chip cookies" (25). In a similar move, the second half of "White Tigers" turns abruptly to recount Maxine's "American life," "a disappointment" in comparison (54). An iconoclastic writer, Kingston cannot bear the mythical discourse of kung fu and the essentialist discourse of China too long before she, mischievously, deflates them.

More than just a matter of impishness, however, "chocolate chip cookies" in the midst of a swordswoman's heroism merges the Chinese and the American contexts and embodies the central theme of destabilization in Kingston. The best example is the woman warrior herself. To fashion a Fa Mu Lan, Kingston ingeniously overlaps her image with the male general Yueh Fei, whose back is believed to be tattooed with patriotic aphorisms. Kingston continues to play on this ambiguity of gender. When Fa Mu Lan becomes pregnant, she has her "armor altered so that I looked like a powerful, big man. . . . Now when I was naked, I was a strange human being indeed — words carved on my back and the baby large in front" (47). By the same token, when Fa Mu Lan declares to the baron that she is the "female avenger" (51), he takes it to mean "a male avenger for women" rather than "a *woman* avenger." The baron then attempts to curry favor "man to man" (51). A furious Fa Mu Lan strips her armor to show him the inscriptions on her back, a bizarre move verging on exhibitionism, which shocks the baron — not so much by the tattooing as by her bare breasts.

Although Fa Mu Lan has to masquerade as a man, these are indeed moments when she displays both genders in the manner of a transvestite, a possibility often ignored by critics. Marjorie Garber's thesis in *Vested Interests: Cross-dressing and Cultural Anxiety* (1992) is enlightening. She maintains that critics tend to "look *through* rather than *at* the cross-dresser, to turn away from a close encounter with the transvestite, and to want instead to subsume that figure within one of the two traditional genders. To elide and erase — or to *appropriate* the transvestite for particular political and critical aims" (9). By corollary, the challenge facing Asian American writers and critics is how to look *at* the sliver of space between the woman warrior's gender roles rather than to look *through* it. In terms of ethnicity, a similar challenge is to hold in view the space called "Asian American," a blank that signifies perennial contestation and negation. The revolutionary potential of the Asian American identity lies precisely in its seeming voidness, a nonessentialized absence that suggests infinite possibilities, provided one is willing to inhabit a perpetual state of flux. But it is symptomatic of the Asian American identity that whatever strategies of self-definition appear to result in a passing, a subsuming into something else. No one can go on fighting forever, including the woman warrior who eventually reverts back to femininity. Even when Kingston's Fa Mu Lan rides into battle with an infant in her armor, few choose to read that as, in the metaphors of gender, a cross-dressing transvestite, or as an Asian American in the making, whose identity depends on infinite oppositions and denials — neither woman nor man, neither Asian nor hegemonic American. Most, Kingston included, see Fa Mu Lan as either a woman, a modern feminist, or as, in Frank Chin's view, a filial-pious, patriarchy-supporting woman in disguise.

Criticism of Kingston constantly reveals the lack of what John Keats describes in a 1817 letter as "Negative Capability," that is, the failure "of being in uncertainties, Mysteries, doubts, without any irritable reaching after fact and reason." One is tempted to resolve ambiguities, especially those concerning pivotal contemporary issues such as gender and ethnicity. Donald Goellnicht, in "Tang Ao in America: Male Subject Positions in *China Men,* " insightfully compares the two initial stories of *The Woman Warrior* and of *China Men* — "No Name Woman" and "On Discovery" — as the founding myths. But he seems to agree with King-Kok Cheung's term in *Articulate Silences* (1993) that such myths deal with "gender reversal" (101) when in fact they imply a third gender or at least gender indeterminacy. The in-between space is hard for anyone to cling to; even Kingston herself is prone to refocus the lens on Fa Mu Lan to do away with the blurred, double vision. This tendency is most strident in Kingston's deployment of pidgin English in its Orientalist mode, hence aligning her narrative with the discursive tradition that belittles Asians. The key phrases "talk-story" and "No Name Woman," for instance, have perfect equivalents in standard English — "storytelling" and "Nameless (or Unnamed) Woman." Similarly, in "White Tigers," the narrator drinks "the snow my fires made run" (30) and accepts those volunteers to her army "with hero-fire in their eyes" (43). In what way are awkward terms such as "made run" and "hero-fire" superior to "melted" and "fire"? Far from defamiliarizing in a Brechtian sense, far from achieving a new level of consciousness via the alienation effect, Kingston's choice of diction, not to mention her plot, brings into being the Orientalist fantasyland resonating with the stilted, stereotypical pidgin, at once comic and exotic.

Pidgin English in Kingston is entirely different from pidgin and foreign languages in Milton Murayama's *All I Asking for Is My Body* (1975), in Louis Chu's *Eat a Bowl of Tea* (1961), and in Wayne Wang's early films *Chan Is Missing* (1981) and *Dim Sum: A Little Bit of Heart* (1985). To Kingston's peers, pidgin and foreign languages are live, dynamic languages, secret codes of sorts shared by their speakers. Whereas Kingston uses pidgin to embellish the exotic, Orientalist ambience of her martial arts fantasies, the others engage it to portray a self-sufficient, though terribly oppressed, community. Whereas Kingston casts her outsider's gaze on pidgin speakers, the others position themselves inside the community, producing texts that often alienate, unapologetically, the "mainstream" audience, particularly through language — Murayama's Hawaii creole, Chu's translation of Cantonese, and Wang's strategic English subtitles to the barrage of Mandarin and Cantonese dialogues.[8]

Youth Culture

Martial metaphors and Asian American literature have largely parted ways since Kingston, except in occasional revivals such as Peter Bacho's *Dark Blue Suit and Other Stories* (1997). The vanishing of warrior imageries in Asian American literature denotes a minority's retreat from the warring 1970s. Increasingly, kung fu has become a part of American youth culture, multiplying in comic books, graphic novels, weekend cartoon shows on TV, toys, video arcades, and movie theaters. Bruce Lee has also been elevated into somewhat of a cult figure in the teen world. Undergoing drastic physical and psychological changes, adolescents yearn to be in control as in an idealized adulthood and to transcend limitations of the body. Teenagers, therefore, are especially susceptible to the kung fu mystique: sudden empowerment via a facile union of the body and the spirit, of the Western self and the Orient. Unlike the counterculture movement in the 1960s spearheaded by the hippies and born in part out of the peace protests, American youth culture revolving around martial symbols embraces rather than rejects the material conditions and the consumer habits in a late-capitalist society. In most cases, middle-class parents purchase these products for their children. For instance, the Sega video game marketed by Sony, *Mortal Kombat Trilogy,* cost about forty dollars at major electronic and video stores across the United States in 1997. But that game has to be mounted on a "PlayStation" (ironic that it is named after "work station") at a retail price of around $150. Outside the home, video games of kung fu motifs are woven into the fabric of an economy of self-perpetuating desire for consumption, and are widely available at video arcades in shopping malls, hotel lobbies, university student unions and dormitories, and roadside cafés — hence occupying public spaces intended for regular social activities. However, the fact that these game rooms are often relegated to the dim, self-enclosed corners of the ground floor of the above-mentioned sites bears out the underground characteristic of such activities, epitomizing the teenage subculture dwelling on the borderline of adult consciousness, a subculture marked by violent and potentially antisocial fantasies. This late-capitalist, corporate culture is, nonetheless, equally adept in gobbling up exotic cultures abroad and deviant behaviors at home. These video games predictably feature a battle between good and evil, between us and them. However brutal the games may be, those phantoms immobilized in front of flickering screens in a cavelike room, those twitching fingers and facial muscles, those schizophrenic reflexes exploding into hoorays when the players score (kill) or into curses when they lose (are killed) serve to work out teenagers' aggressiveness, offering the illusion of control, neutralizing dissent, inculcating the ideological consensus of the one and only consumerist lifestyle.

Compared to the underworld inhabited by urban black youths in Henry Giroux's *Fugitive Cultures* (1996), video games are tamer by far and fraught with hegemonic interpellation. Giroux defines youth as

> inhabit[ing] many fronts ranging across the cultures of the mall,
> computer bulletin boards, rock music, gangsta rap, urban basketball

courts, hacker coffee shops, and an urban underground where sex is
traded, drugs exchanged, politics created, and sexuality expressed. These
are sites of fugitive cultures not because they are inherently oppositional . . .
but because they often do not conform to the imperatives of adults and
mainstream culture. Youth as a self and social construction has become
indeterminate, alien, and sometimes hazardous in the public eye. (10–11)

What Giroux is concerned with harks back to, shall we say, Bruce Lee's
initial fans in the 1970s. Decades later, the middle-class users of video
games are enormously privileged and domesticated, albeit as susceptible
as ever to delusions of grandeur.

Yet even experts disagree on whether video games induce or elimi-
nate violent impulses. Randy Schroeder, in "Playspace Invaders: Huizinga,
Baudrillard and Video Game Violence," attests that "three seminal studies
on arcade games in 1983 . . . all failed to establish any significant correlation between video game-playing and negative behavior" (145). Nevertheless, Schroeder concedes that dialogue with the video game is, as noted
by Eugene F. Provenzo Jr., "defined primarily by the computer and the
way it has been programmed" and not by the player's imagination
(Schroeder 144).

Without trying to resolve the complex issue, let me turn now to a
specific example of video games — *Mortal Kombat*.[9] There are, of course,
hundreds of other games featuring kung fu motifs, almost all of them
kaleidoscopically configured in American youth culture through an array
of forms.[10] More widely accepted than *Mortal Kombat* is perhaps the
comical *Teenage Mutant Ninja Turtles,* considered to be more wholesome family entertainment. As bloody as our subject at hand, though
less profitable, is *Street Fighter,* which was turned into a film in 1994,
starring Jean-Claude Van Damme and Raul Julia. Obviously, those famous video games without an overt kung fu theme are excluded, such
as Nintendo's *Super Mario Bros.*

Mortal Kombat manifests itself as video games, as cartoon shows, and
as a full-length feature film in 1996. Although video games seem to pre-
cede the other two forms of production, *Mortal Kombat* the game is itself a reproduction of a sci-fi, kung fu fantasy and thus enjoys minimal
originary status. Jean Baudrillard's contention that simulation is "the
generation by models of a real without origin or reality: a hyperreal"
(1) explicates perfectly the lineage, or the lack thereof, of *Mortal Kombat*.
The poorest reincarnation of the trinity is the cartoon, made specifi-

cally for the promotion of the film as well as related products, such as Web page, Crew T-shirt, tour, practice kit, book, and Kombat Klub in Los Angeles. Almost every cultural production, particularly in the electronic media, is exploited by the company to cast as wide a net as possible. The target group of consumers is undoubtedly children, adolescents, and young adults, as the plot, tempo, characters, and language of the game and the film mirror those of the youth culture.

The story of the *Mortal Kombat* is necessarily simplistic, even somewhat archetypal. Through a martial arts tournament called Mortal Kombat, mortals defend the Earth against the "hostile takeover" by the sorcerer Shang Tsung and other evil figures from the Outworld. Violence is posed not only as a problem-solving tool but as a mission to ensure the survival of the Earth. To achieve the noble goal of self-preservation, much blood is spilled. But the "Game Konfigure" in the instruction manual explains that blood can be turned off. When it is turned off, the "Finishing Moves" of beheading or killing with blood splashed all over the screen cannot be performed. A self-contradictory logic, one suspects that the option of no-blood, no-win is incorporated into the computer program to fend off charges of excessive violence. It is, in effect, an admission of excessive violence. The "Game Konfigure" also allows the player to choose the sorcerer Shang Tsung's Morphs, or transformations into another image, hence increasing the thrill of the game.

With the logo of a coiling dragon superimposed on the box containing the video game, on every single page of the instruction manual, and on the video images of the game itself, *Mortal Kombat* oozes such Orientalist fetishes. All the warriors fight with kung fu postures, dressed in quasi-Chinese or quasi-Japanese costumes. Equipped with biographies in the instruction manual, many characters have Asian-sounding names. The Chinese cast includes Liu Kang, the Warrior Monk (whose simulated image is the most Asian of all the characters); Kung Lao; Shao Kahn (named after Genghis Khan, despite the slightly varied spellings); Jade; and Shang Tsung (complete with Fu Manchu's goatees in the cartoon). The Japanese contingent includes Smoke (Cyber-Ninja); Kitana (who throws her folding fans like deadly boomerangs); Motaro (half-human, half-beast); Kintaro; and Prince Goro. The last two are monsters with four arms each. The character "Sheeva" descends from the Hindu god of destruction, Shiva. The "Earth's sworn protector," Rayden, though his name can be construed as Western, always appears with a samurai staff and hat worn low to cover his eyes.[11] Not to completely alienate American consumers, there are, in addition to Liu Kang, two mortal combatants readily recognizable by American teens — the surfer-type movie star Johnny Cage and the blonde Sonya Blade. Moreover, advertising gimmicks so promiscuous in today's market are evident in the substitutions of "C's" with "K's," as in "Mortal *K*ombat Trilogy." Changes of spellings are believed to be eye-catching, for they disrupt the reading process.

There are thirty-two warriors in Mortal Kombat Trilogy, a substantially larger cast than the meager seven in Mortal Kombat I. The basic moves of each of the combatants consist of "Klose Quarters (the Elbow, the Knee and the Throw)," "Special Moves," "Krouching Moves (primarily for defense)," "Spinning Moves (the Roundhouse Kick and the Foot Sweep)," and "Aerial Moves (Flying Punches and Kicks)." Most warriors have their unique combat skills, exemplified by Kitana's fans and Liu Kang's flying kicks. The latter is a series of kicks performed while Liu Kang glides horizontally in the air as if treading on his opponent. The misleading instruction on "Special Moves" is the basis for the marketing strategies: "These moves, whether Special Kicks or Elemental Bolts, make the Mortal Kombat Warriors the fiercest and most ferocious Kombatants around. Mastering their special moves will make you the same." The last line exposes the illusion of control and the player's identification with visual images that lie at the heart of the fascination with video games. By the same token, the mathematical combination of these moves with the number of warriors creates the appearance of multiple options, of variety, when, in reality, they are repetitions. A close look at the images and the biographies of the thirty-two warriors in the instruction manual reveals that, except in blatant cases such as the four-arm grotesque Goro, they are somewhat alike, with good and bad characters nearly indistinguishable.

The film *Mortal Kombat* (1996) is directed by Paul Anderson and filmed in Thailand. This film has one of the longest concluding credits to list its special-effects teams. Growing out of the sci-fi bent of the video game, many filmic sequences are computer-generated and digitized, hence involving a huge team of technicians. As the credits roll, the sound track repeats its theme music, a fast-paced, MTV-style electronic piece dominated by synthesizers and punctuated by shouts of "Mortal Kombat" and an incantation of the names of the characters. Once again, the deep, husky voice recites the names indiscriminately. Virtue and evil are flattened and entwined, no matter how three-dimensional the characters may look in virtual reality.

The film focuses on the trio Liu Kang, Johnny Cage, and Sonya Blade. Liu (Americanized as Lu or perhaps Lou) Kang is played by the Hong Kong actor Robin Shou, who also doubles as the martial arts choreographer. In general, the film is heavily derivative of the video game, including commands such as "Finish him!" or "fatality." One strain of the film does stand out from its predecessor: the film romanticizes the self in the most adolescent and egotistic way. The finale of the defeat of Shang Tsung is predicated on Liu Kang's ability to face three types of fears. He must confront the fear of enemies, the fear of himself, and the fear of his own destiny. Abstract and vacuous, the last ordeal suggests that Liu Kang should rid himself of the sense of guilt over the death of his brother Chen at the hands of Shang Tsung years before. Liu has since fled from his obligation of avenging his brother to America, an escapist solution that any average teenager (or even adult) is likely to embrace. Liu Kang, in other words, is urged to take no responsibility for the death of his brother, who, in Liu's words, "took his own path." This kind of feel-good, Gen-X justification for egotism somehow leads Liu to prevail over Shang Tsung. The film perpetuates the ideology of unrestrained individualism, one marked by boundless delusion of heroism and absolutely no personal accountability. The genre of teen kung fu films relentlessly recycles such an ideology in *The Karate Kid, Best of the Best, Surf Ninjas, Sidekicks,* and innumerable other flicks, including sequels to the aforementioned ones.

In a transnational economy, it is a moot point to quibble over whether Sega-Sony products such as *Mortal Kombat Trilogy* are made in America, Japan, or elsewhere. The intricacies of corporate contracts as well as the ever-changing negotiations among businesses are beyond the purview of this chapter. According to Kevin Maney's *Megamedia Shakeout* (1995), *Mortal Kombat* was initially developed by Sega, a company founded by an American in Tokyo, with the home base in Japan and the U.S. division in Redwood City, California (329). This video game is only one of Sega's whole arsenal of, in the words of Randy Schroeder, "hard-hitting" games to penetrate Nintendo's monopoly of the industry in the 1980s and 1990s.[12] Conversely, Nintendo was founded by the Yamauchi family in Japan and its U.S. subsidiary, Nintendo of America, is located in Redmond, Washington. Despite the predominantly Anglo-American names for the team that created *Mortal Kombat Trilogy,* the video game bears the Sony logo and is marketed by Sony. If one insists that the Orientalist stereotypes in the game are the brainchild of the Anglo-American team, a Japanese company finances the production and oversees the distribution. In terms of consumption of such merchandise, the picture is equally blurred. During the holiday seasons in industrialized countries around the globe, these games are frantically awaited by long lines of, mostly, parents, Asian or otherwise. Ultimately, martial metaphors embodied by Bruce Lee, Maxine Hong Kingston, and *Mortal Kombat* have become universal. Historical ties do not equal exclusive rights; indeed, no one can enjoy a proprietary relationship to any specific aspect of culture. Yet even if a minority is willing to share its cultural heritage, these metaphors at times return to haunt members of that group, which is what happened in the death of Vincent Chin.

CHAPTER FOUR

Vincent Chin and Baseball

Law, Racial Violence, and Masculinity

When the news of Vincent Chin's death reached Juanita, wife of Ronald Ebens, she saw no point in informing her husband, a white foreman at work at a Detroit automobile factory. She added during the interview in the eighty-two-minute PBS program "Who Killed Vincent Chin?" (1988) that her husband in fact came home late that evening because he played on a baseball team every Thursday. This passing reference provided a horrifying revelation for the viewers, for on June 19, 1982, or four days before his death, Chin was involved in a barroom brawl at Fancy Pants Lounge, a nude dancing establishment in Highland Park, Detroit, with Ronald Ebens and his stepson Michael Nitz, who later jointly stalked Chin for at least half an hour and then bludgeoned him to death with a baseball bat. She apparently did not wish to spoil Ronald Ebens's night out, a game of leisure utilizing their weapon of choice. Such recreational activity led one to postulate that Ebens did not suffer from post-traumatic stress disorder (PTSD) that should have kept him from associating with baseball for some time to come.

The eerie connection between the killing and baseball went beyond the murder weapon. Ronald Ebens at one point in "Who Killed Vincent Chin?" mused that the incident would not have taken place had he "had an accident" himself or gone to "a ball game." Ebens and Nitz were clearly equipped for both activities at the baseball diamond and outside Fancy Pants. When the scuffle extended itself to the nude bar's parking lot, Ebens "opened [Nitz's] hatchback and removed a baseball bat" (*United States v. Ronald Ebens*, 800 F.2d at 1428, [1986]), as if getting ready to "play ball."[1] What Ebens failed to perceive was that the two endeavors were one and the same. Ebens was *in fact* playing baseball, swinging at a human head "like a baseball player swinging for a home run, full of contact, full of impact," as Officer Morris Cotton at the crime scene described the murder in "Who Killed Vincent Chin?"

However, baseball *is* the national pastime. Michael S. Kimmel notes that "Baseball is sport as American pastoral ... baseball is a metaphor for America" (55). It seems fitting that Ebens and Nitz would take out their frustration in the American way — first punishing a "little motherfucker" allegedly responsible for American automobile employees' being "out of work" as a result of "Japanese imports" (the dancer Racine Colwell's testimony of Ebens's racial slurs *prior to* the fistfight) and, days later, working out as a means of relaxation. On a personal level, the crime itself was committed amid a happy hour with liquor and nude dancers, the world of play where one vented pent-up emotions from a long day's work. Sexual violence was already implicit at the site of entertainment, just as potential violence lurked not far beneath any close and hotly contested game in sports. On a collective level, the 1980s was punctuated by massive layoffs in the auto industry and the resulting Japan bashing, the most concrete images of which were those of sledgehammers smashing Japanese cars' windshields. Despite Ebens's attorney Frank Easman's claim that it is "a quantum leap, a giant jump" to link the bashing of Japanese cars to the bashing of Chin, it is but a small step in imagination to conjure up various blunt objects capable of delivering brute force — baseball bat, sledgehammer, gunboat diplomacy, *Madame Butterfly*'s or *Miss Saigon*'s Yankee lover. Racial violence, to be sure, never erupts in a vacuum. It is not a deviation from, but a natural outgrowth of, its cultural context.

As painful as it is for Asian Americans to even recall the name of Vincent Chin, this revisiting of a race-motivated murder nearly two decades ago is made imperative in the wake of the violence against Rodney King, Reginald Denny, Nicole Brown, and other related incidents. Although these latter victims and the ensuing trials received full-blown media coverage, Chin never quite registered in the consciousness of the American public, a sad commentary on the invisibility of the "hardworking," "uncomplaining" model minority. Minority critics have devoted some attention to this crime, though. Masao Miyoshi touches on the connection between Japan bashing in the Reagan era and Chin's murder (*Off*

Center 63); Yen Le Espiritu investigates how the Chin case contributes to an Asian American panethnicity (*Asian American Panethnicity* 141–57); a Web site on the Internet is devoted to the incident and its legacy; the Rashomonesque program "Who Killed Vincent Chin?" montages the killers showing no remorse and the victim's mother pleading for justice.

But beyond these attempts, few critical studies on the Vincent Chin case have been undertaken; no one in fact has tried to situate this transgression squarely in the context of American culture. Indeed, the crime and the trial are viewed as an aberration from American democracy and justice. Yet could one be so naive as to suggest that the transgressiveness of a Mr. Hyde unleashed by, to borrow from Georges Bataille's *Eroticism* (1962), "the world of play" is somehow divorced from a Dr. Jekyll? Isn't the Ebens who wielded the bat on June 19, 1982, the same man who swung for a home run on the following Thursday evening? Isn't Chin's death Ebens's home run? The troubling intersection of legal injustice, racial difference, masculinity in sports, and sexploitation maps out a dark recess of the American psyche, with violence being instantly activated by a crisis perceived as having been caused by the other. This other is anyone deemed alien in the midst of a paranoiac culture; this other is the defenseless scapegoat against whom anger can be vented with impunity. The sharp division between the subject and the object (self versus other), or between a particular facet of the subject and the rest of it, lies not only in the culture that engendered the perpetration but in the law that was supposed to redress the wrong. Both the prosecution and the defense approached the Chin case on the same ideological foundation of distinct divisions. Finally, the scandalous legal injustice of the case cannot be fully grasped if one fails to study the issues of race, sports, and sex—areas that are constructed on bases as epistemologically dualistic as the law. Although it is far from my intention and capability to write a legal treatise on the Chin case, this cultural critique must begin from the specificities of trial documents and then branch out to American culture as a whole.

Law

The ghost of Vincent Chin does not rest in peace (figure 24). After the light sentence of three years' probation and three thousand-dollar fine was meted out to the defendants by Wayne County Circuit Court Judge Charles Kaufman on March 16, 1983, the U.S. Department of Justice an-

Figure 24. Vincent Chin, bludgeoned to death in 1982.

nounced on November 2, 1983, grand jury indictments against Ebens and Nitz for violations of Chin's civil rights. One of the most effective pressure groups forcing the federal government's involvement was American Citizens for Justice (ACJ), officially founded on March 31, 1983, by the Asian American community in response to the light sentencing. In June 1984, a federal jury convicted Ebens of the civil rights charges but acquitted Nitz. Federal judge Anna Diggs Taylor sentenced Ebens to twenty-five years in prison. However, a three-judge panel of the U.S. Court of Appeals for the Sixth Circuit reversed and remanded the conviction of Ebens on September 11, 1986. A change of venue to the "Southern District of Ohio" was granted on February 23, 1987, because of "saturation publicity" "throughout Michigan and the Northern District of Ohio" (*Ebens*, 654 F. Supp at 144). A jury in Cincinnati found Ebens not guilty on May 1, 1987.

Trials are legal practices that stress factual evidence. Theoretical reflections, general observations, and speculative arguments are likely to be dismissed in a court of law. Throughout the trials, major players of the legal proceedings manipulated this principle of facticity to their respective advantages. Defense attorneys, for instance, sought to isolate the crime from, rather than to read it as part of, the defendants' lives and the culture in which they live. To fuse a single act with a culture clearly required much more than a positivist approach to what was said and done for the duration of that act. Therefore, the defense contended that the assault was a deviation from the defendants' lives, an unpremeditated tragic accident as a result of alcohol, carelessness, and happenstance. This argument certainly convinced Judge Kaufman, who defended his lenient sentence by pointing out the defendants' "stable working backgrounds and lack of criminal records." "You don't make the punishment fit the crime," Kaufman added, "you make the punishment fit the criminal'" (qtd. in Espiritu 141). In the same offhanded fashion, Kaufman asserted: "Had this been a brutal murder, of course these fellows would be in jail now" ("Who Killed Vincent Chin?"). According to his definition of brutality, Ebens and Nitz merely *strayed away from* their apparent normalcy. Judge Kaufman agreed with defense attorneys that the act and its agents were so incongruous that the latter were taken to be, *in normal circumstances*, incapable of committing such a crime, one viewed by Kaufman as not "a brutal murder."

Testifying on his own mental state at the moment of the attack, Ebens tried to use the same strategy of the compartmentalization of personality:

> When I seen him [Chin] scuffling [with Nitz after being clubbed a few times by Ebens but having gotten loose], it just flashed in my mind. He is going to get hurt again, and I started toward him, and it was almost audible to me, and something just snapped. I don't remember from there on what did happened [*sic*]. (*US v. RE,* No. 83-60629-CR, vol. 289, p. 184; for citation of references, see note 1.)

Whether they were carefully rehearsed or not, Ebens's descriptions contained no clearly defined agent of action. The "I" did nothing more than "seen" and "started toward him," followed by the beating, which kind of just manifested itself. Ebens portrayed himself not as the agent but as the vehicle/conduit of the crime, propelled less by his own rage than by a collection of amorphous forces — a "flash" of something, an intuition that someone was about to "get hurt," and certain "snap[ping]" sound. Ebens implied that he should not have been held accountable for what transpired *after* the blackout of his faculties — a common strategy of insanity defense.

By casting the alleged loss of control in auditory rather than visual terms, the defendant emphasized that the attack occurred unexpectedly and inadvertently. Of the human senses, sight was the one most often

relied on: one could hold something in one's gaze for an extended period of time. In comparison, "to prick up one's ears" hardly came close
to the intensity of a visual inspection. On the other hand, one could
choose *not* to look by closing one's eyes, whereas ears remained open at
all times. Because of the perpetual stimulations on one's eardrums, hearing becomes a sense so ordinary that it registers less on consciousness
than seeing does. Ebens therefore not only compartmentalized his killing
self from his usual self, but he was crafty enough to provide only a ten-
uous link between the two. The metaphor of hearing served to insulate
himself from the crime, as the human sense considered somewhat removed from the core of consciousness was presented as the sole detec-
tor of the imminent assault.

Ebens's auditory rather than visual metaphor ("It was almost audible to me") may have arisen from his experiences of baseball. A batter
or the spectators close to the plate would at times come to realize, in-
stantaneously, that a bat had splintered against the pitch more by the
piercing pop than by the sight of a slightly cracked bat. Ebens heard the
"almost audible" ring of his mind cracking in the same way the hitter
or, better still for Ebens's defense, the bystander would discern the splitting of a bat. Baseball is so integral a part of Ebens that even his court-
room performance seeking to isolate the night of the beating from the
rest of his life in effect resorts to one of his favorite activities in life: the
lingo and images of sports. (A discussion of sports follows in the section titled "Balls and Beers.")

Because the defendants had pleaded guilty to manslaughter, Kaufman's
sentence, as preposterous as it was, practically blocked them from being tried again. The U.S. Department of Justice stepped in under mounting pressure from the media and the Asian American community. The
only way for the federal government to reopen the case was to charge
the defendants with violating the civil rights of Vincent Chin. Yet, by definition, prosecutors of civil rights violation cases must prove beyond any
reasonable doubt that the crime was racially motivated, as civil rights
statutes were designed "to protect any person because of his race, color,
religion or national origin from intimidation . . . in enjoyment of facilities . . . or entertainment which serves the public." A civil rights case
differs from a criminal case in that the fact of a criminal act, such as the
slaying of Vincent Chin, does not constitute reason for conviction. Only
by proving the *racial* intent of that act could the prosecutor win a con-

viction. The distinction surfaced in attorney Liza Chan's advice to three prosecution witnesses: "The question is not whether it is a murder or justifiable, the question is whether there was any reason that they— Vincent was bothered at all, let alone killed, because of his race, bothered from enjoying the services and entertainment because of his race" (*US v. RE*, 800 F.2d, p. 1443).

In order to prove racial motivation in a court of law, the prosecutors' options were severely limited, which led to the heavy emphasis on verbal expressions pertaining to race, something extremely difficult to pinpoint in the midst of a chaotic barroom brawl. In the heat of an argument and physical struggle, with participants shrouded by a cacophony of loud music and noise, blinded by the strobe light and swaying nude bodies, affected by alcohol, adrenaline, and exhaustion, it was nearly impossible to construct an event that could be shown to be indisputably racist. Even verbal abuse and physical contact could be construed by different people in entirely different ways. Beyond spoken words, much was deemed too subtle and unreliable as evidence, such as public sentiment, general atmosphere, or even body language.

Remarks made at the scene on the spur of the moment were not the only difficult thing to verify. In the effort to establish a history of racial prejudice, the government committed the blunder of presenting Willie Davis, an African American who claimed that a blond man resembling Ebens had hurled racial epithets at him in a Detroit bar in 1974, nearly a decade before the crime. The remove of time, Davis's inability to positively identify Ebens, and the forced linkages of African and Asian races weakened Davis's testimony. This botched attempt to incriminate Ebens betrayed how woefully inadequate federal prosecutors were in recognizing the specific problems facing Asian Americans.

Compounding the difficulties were the witnesses' self-interest and relationship with the defendants or the victim, rendering their testimony far from "the truth...and nothing but the truth." The dancer Racine Colwell, a government witness, testified that Ebens shouted across the dance stage at Chin: "It's because [of] you little mother fuckers that we're out of work." Chin replied: "I'm not a little mother fucker." Ebens countered: "Well, I'm not sure if you're a big one or a little one" (*US v. RE*, No. 83-60629-CR, vol. 299, p. 226), which led Chin to go around the stage to confront Ebens. The defense argued that even in Colwell's damaging testimony, no racial slurs were used by Ebens, which would only stand if one refused to read any racial implication into the references to layoffs in automobile plants and to "*little* mother fucker" (my emphasis). The defense also suggested that Colwell might be biased because she had known Chin previously while working at another nude bar.

The crucial moments that culminated in the fight were represented in a very different light by the defense. David N. Lawson, Ebens's attorney, maintained that Ebens did nothing more than verbally respond to Chin's provocation: "Big fucker, little fucker, we're all fuckers" (*US v. RE*, No. 83-60629-CR, vol. 299, p. 23). Yet a third version of the same episode emerged. The dancer Starlene, a defense witness, asserted that the fight started when she declined to be tipped by Chin, who wanted to put bills in her "costume." Starlene claimed that she had just started her career and that she did not wish to be touched. Ebens came to her rescue and called Chin "a boy," adding: "you don't know a good thing ["pussy" by another account] when you see one," to which Chin replied: "I'm not a boy." The government later called a witness who alleged that Starlene allowed Ebens to "go down on her," a slang in that circle for (simulated?) oral sex, during her performance, hence shedding doubt on the impartiality of Starlene's testimony. The U.S. District Court of Appeals, Sixth Circuit, which decided to reverse and remand Ebens's sentence of twenty-five years, seemed to find the prosecution's line of argument on oral sex repulsive and unfairly damaging to the witness's credibility. But if the report of Starlene's accuser could be substantiated, which would not be hard to do as the act was designed for public consumption, Starlene's behavior would not only contradict her statement about not letting Chin touch her for the reason she stated but would call into question the mild form of squabble over the usage of "boy" Starlene related. While viewing the allegation against Starlene as an example of "prosecutorial misconduct," the court of appeals may have itself misbehaved in blocking a legitimate move to impeach a key defense witness.

Race

The defense attorneys tried to divorce the crime not only from the criminal but from any appearance of race hate in this multiracial society, evident from defense attorney Easman's remark about the "quantum leap" from resentment against Japanese import cars to violence against an Asian American. The total erasure of race in the incident was an absurd contention. Ebens was cited at Fancy Pants as calling Chin a "Chink," a "Nip," and "making remarks about foreign car imports" (*US v. RE*, 800 F.2d, p. 1427). While driving around the block to hunt down Chin and his friend Jimmy Choi, the father and the stepson picked up a Jimmy Perry, and offered him twenty dollars for his assistance in "catching a 'Chinese guy' and 'busting his head' " (*US v. RE*, 800 F.2d, p. 1428). True, most of this testimony was disputed or denied by defense witnesses, including Ebens and Nitz. However, Ebens admitted that he told Perry that he "was looking for two orientals" (*US v. RE*, No. 83-60629-CR, vol. 289, p. 179). Assuming all the testimonies were false except Ebens's own sworn statement, at least one could deduce that Ebens was aware of racial difference, so much so that race became the "scent" to be picked up by the hound. To identify Chin and Choi as Orientals, a deeply racist term born out of imperialism, was already wrong because they were as American as Ebens and Nitz. Moreover, one could conclude that even if Ebens had mistaken Chin to be a Japanese at Fancy Pants, it was the Oriental other that Ebens was after on the street.

The host of racial epithets involving both Japanese and Chinese that the defendants reportedly used against Chin recalled Rene Girard's argument in *Scapegoat* (1986). Girard examined "persecution texts" of ancient myths and medieval accounts written by "naive persecutors" and detected four types or stages of stereotype that culminated in persecution.[2] Girard's most insightful observation lay in the fact that a prerequisite for scapegoating someone or a group was the obliteration of differences among potential victims, who were identified by some physical handicap or foreignness. All Asians and things Asian were lumped together in this incident, epitomized by imported Japanese cars. These alien scapegoats came to represent the cause of Ebens's problems. Furthermore, Ebens was bent on tracking down Chin and his friend Choi. To achieve this, he even asked, outside the bar, the other two members of Chin's party—Koivu and Sirosky, both white—where Chin and Choi were. Race evidently dictated Ebens's choice of quarry. His fury expanded from Chin to include someone "like" Chin, but not Koivu and Sirosky, people "like" the Ebenses. (Incidentally, all three of Chin's friends were equally involved in extricating Chin, Ebens, and Nitz during the scuffle.) But if race was used at all by the defense, it was used to exonerate Ebens. The defense alleged that Chin failed to properly tip the African American stripper, Starlene, while handsomely tipping a white stripper. The defense strategy was to turn Chin into a racist favoring white dancers, which triggered the fight with Ebens, an outraged "antiracist" — a common yet vicious legal maneuveur of accusing the victim of a crime of being the *cause* of the crime.

On the other hand, the prosecution and the media sought to narrow the case by portraying the homicide solely as an instance of racial violence perpetrated by discontented autoworkers against someone mistaken for being Japanese. Although Girard's insights could be used to dissect the crime, such a theoretical approach would have no impact legally and would contribute minimally to newsworthiness. This constricted interpretation of an anti-Japanese crime was undertaken for political motives, just like the defense attorneys' denial of any connection to racially motivated crimes. Both approaches were extreme and distorted the true contours of the incident. Much weight then was given to Ebens's statement about "Japanese imports" and widespread unemployment. For instance, in "Who Killed Vincent Chin?" a member of the first civil rights violation trial jury, which as a body found Ebens guilty, referred to Racine Colwell's testimony that the defendant said "It's because [of] you little mother fuckers that we're out of work" as the key in swaying the jury's decision. That remark allegedly made by Ebens exposed the xenophobia of the 1980s.

At the same time, by zooming in on anti-Japanese sentiment, this approach failed to anatomize the "mistake" over ethnic identity, a mistake resulting from the stereotype that "all Asians look alike." To call this a mistake suggested that Chin could have averted Ebens's wrath had he somehow identified himself as Chinese, which would also be wrong for he was an American. But such self-identification is often beyond the reach of victims of racial crimes assumed to be someone they are not. In addition, the public rhetoric of "mistaken identity" was articulated on the premise that a number of blue-collar workers were so ignorant and bigoted as to make such a mistake, whereas the larger society went about business as usual, secure in its self-image of broad-mindedness. The narrowness of both the legal and the media approaches demonstrated the need to sequester the crime within a certain segment of the population rather than risk implicating the totality of American culture.

But the inverse of the theory of mistaken identity raises alarming questions: because all Asians look alike, any Asian-looking person will do as the punching bag for white wrath. As such, one reaches the terrifying conclusion that average Americans, to use Kaufman's words, marked by "stable working backgrounds and lack of criminal records," harbor a readiness to persecute the scapegoat. To borrow Hannah Arendt's thesis in *Eichmann in Jerusalem* (1963), evil is not located in the metaphysical realm of the demonic but in the physical being of the banal—one as commonplace as Ronald Ebens who, with his twin passion for sports and female nudity, would explode one night and kill.

Yet the Asian American community itself contributed to this narrow interpretation of the crime. The reversal of Ebens's twenty-five year sentence handed down by the court of appeals hinged on what the three-judge panel termed "prosecutorial misconduct" and an audiotape of attorney Liza Chan allegedly coaching and rehearsing the three key government witnesses—Choi, Koivu, and Sirosky. The Chan tape had previously been ruled by Judge Taylor inadmissible on hearsay grounds; the defense attorneys were only allowed to cite from the transcript of the tape. The court of appeals deemed the content of the tape so critical in its decision that it included excerpts from the tape as Appendix A to its ruling. The three-page appendix demonstrated that Liza Chan, as an attorney working for the Chin family, blatantly attempted to coordinate the memories of the three witnesses in line with the civil rights charges. The interview focused on two kinds of statements Ebens supposedly made: racial slurs (such as "Chink") in relation to foreign imports; and obscenities such as "motherfuckers." The first type clearly veered toward the racial motivation of the slaughter, and the second pointed toward the infringement of Chin's civil rights on the grounds that obscenities prevented Chin from "enjoyment of facilities . . . or entertainment which serves the public." Problems were already developing in the taped interview when one or two of the three witnesses could not quite remember the exact racial slurs or curses that the other witness or that Chan herself put forward. This incongruity occurred despite Chan's admonitions at the outset that "[w]hen it's a federal prosecution, h'm, we're all going to have to be agreeing on this is what happened. Now, if you don't agree, like I explained to them earlier, you definitely remembered certain things happened . . . other than that [a hypothetical discrepancy provided by Chan], let's all have it sort of down, have it down pat." This unnerved Koivu so much that he asked: "Is there any harm in getting too accurate, because they could say, well, you all rehersed [*sic*] this?" (*US v. RE*, 800 F.2d, p. 1443).

Koivu's concern, quoted by the defense in cross-examination, sabotaged his own testimony. The court of appeals likewise used Koivu to justify its reversal. It was sad that Liza Chan's effort eventually undermined the case, considering what she had done as the crusader for Vincent Chin. She was one of the pivotal figures in the founding of ACJ, in rallying Asian American community in the greater Detroit area, and in attracting media and public support. Chan was so formidable an opponent that in its opening statement the defense hinted that a single attorney's campaign was the driving force behind the Ebens trial.

Balls and Beers

Not only is a "ball" the round object used in athletic competitions, but "balls" refers to testicles, masculinity, or "guts." The construction of the masculine gender rests on the demonstration of manly prowess, prominently and regularly displayed in sports in American culture. A Caucasian American male thus achieves his identity in relation to the others who do not possess commensurate qualities — women and weaker men, including males of other races. Because "civilized" men no longer go head-hunting in the woods, such flaunting of manhood is relegated to realms of "ritualized aggression" such as sports.[3] The word *ritual* often evokes associations of primordial urges and primitive practices. But sports are thoroughly modernized rituals with huge business machinery orchestrating each televised and commodified game. These modern rituals customarily entail, in the company Ebens and Nitz kept (if not extending to the rest of the population), the consumption of alcoholic beverages and of female sexuality. Balls and beers intertwine, after a baseball game, at a topless bar.[4]

The thin line between sports and violence, as well as their underlying linkages to masculinity, has been explored by various critics. Douglas A. Noverr and Lawrence E. Ziewacz, in "Violence in American Sports," describe "ballparks and sports arenas" as "places where healthy and energetic males 'let off steam'" (132). They reinforce this description in the conclusion to their essay: "identification with" sports violence "allowed the passive, middle-class American a chance to safely rid himself of bottled-up violence and hostility" (144). The use of the masculine gender here suggests that professional sports are the domain of male athletes and fans. Kendall Blanchard, in *The Anthropology of Sport: An Introduction,* also observes that "sport competition has been dubbed . . .

as war without weapons and battle without bullets.... In a reverse of that image, war can also be seen as a sort of game" (240).

Despite Michael S. Kimmel's eulogy of baseball as "a metaphor for America" cited earlier, his analysis of the growth of baseball around the turn of the twentieth century illustrates the fact that baseball arose as a reaction to the threat to masculinity posed by nonwhite immigrants and women. "While providing the illusion of equality and offering organized leisure-time distraction, as well as by shaping working-class masculinity as constituted by its superiority over women [as well as nonwhites, who were initially excluded from baseball], baseball helped white working-class men accommodate themselves to the emergent order" (64).

On the stand, both Ebens and Nitz bore witness, unwittingly, to such a complex interlocking of sports, violence, and masculinity. Responding to the defense attorney's leading question, Ebens said that it was a "habit" of his to go and have a beer after work (*US v. RE*, No. 83-60629-CR, vol. 289, p. 154), although the defense did not get into what kind of place beers were purchased and consumed. From Ebens's statements elsewhere, we learn that it was common for Ebens to play baseball and frequent a bar after work. In fact, so immersed was Ebens in this blue-collar lifestyle so typical in Michigan and other heavily industrialized Midwestern states that he once owned and operated a bar called "Ron's Place" in Detroit.

All the trappings of "manliness" — sports, alcohol, female bodies — were regrettable but perhaps unavoidable. A friend of Ebens's at Chrysler — like Ebens, from a small town in Wisconsin — revealed on the witness stand and in "Who Killed Vincent Chin?" that after work they used to go hunting in Wisconsin, a lifestyle denied them in urban Detroit. However, male aggressiveness must somehow be vented, if not through shooting and butchering animals, then through sports, alcohol, and commodified female bodies. Ebens tried to sustain this delusion of masculine power in "the world of play" because in "the world of work" he was a mere Chrysler foreman at the mercy of national and international economic forces. His stepson Nitz, for example, had been laid off by an auto plant a few years before the encounter with Chin. The fear of economic instability fueled their xenophobia, because scapegoating imported Japanese cars and "aliens" such as Chin outside of work seemed to be a more effective way to secure a sense of control than taking on and bringing about changes in the capitalist system at the work-place.

With regard to the stepson's testimony, Nitz stated that he "used to go to the Booby Trap [a topless bar] by Soft Ball City [in Detroit] after the games" (*US v. RE*, No. 83-60629-CR, vol. 282, p. 65). Nitz played softball, baseball, and other sports himself. All of Nitz's character wit-nesses vouched that the Michael Nitz they coached, played on the team with, or befriended at the high school in Clinton, Wisconsin, was a good athlete who was incapable of telling a lie. The defense surely spent some time arranging for the appearances of these various character witnesses, who, after graduating with Nitz from high school, had left for other re-gions of the United States for jobs. Such character testimony was de-signed to disprove the connection between an athletic, teenage Nitz and a violent, older Nitz. The irony, however, was that if one refuted the the-sis of compartmentalization of individual psyche and of culture, what Nitz's high school acquaintances had professed actually underscored the chilling contiguity between ordinary Americanness and malice toward what was perceived to be un-American.[5]

To protect minorities from the dominant group, the architects of the civil rights statute seem to have predicted that violence against minori-ties is less likely to erupt at the workplace where personal preferences are held in check than in sites of after-work entertainment. In these public locations — ballparks and bars, for example — one is supposed to relax and let one's guard down. Ugly prejudices can then surface. The fact that Chin, an "Oriental," was enjoying himself and generously tip-ping American dancers aroused Ebens's rage.[6] It was Chin's tragic fate that his role switched from being a hunter to being the hunted; he should have been aware that his skin color doomed him as one of the subal-terns in American culture.

Last Words

Dr. Jeffrey Lawrence Crecilius, neurosurgery resident at Henry Ford Hos-pital, evaluated Chin on that fatal night and testified in court that Chin suffered from "swelling of his head. Two lacerations, or open wounds of the scalp [on the left side at the back of his head]. He also had some abrasions about his shoulders, upper chest, and neck. His neurologic function was such that all that was remaining to function properly was that he was breathing" (*US v. RE*, No. 83-60629-CR, vol. 229, p. 117). Chin was reported to have been in a "deep coma" upon arrival at the hospital and to have never regained consciousness before the life-support system was removed.

The Asian American community's ensuing outrage was frequently channeled through Vincent Chin's alleged "dying words while in the arms of his friend Jimmy Choi": "It isn't fair" ("The Case for Vincent Chin" 1). These words appeared as the title of ACJ's official statement on the Chin case; they were on the banners of various demonstrations; they were often the headline for newspaper articles on Chin. It was unclear where exactly Choi heard these words—at the crime scene or in the ambulance. (A coma would naturally preclude the possibility of Chin making such a coherent, pointed comment on his state of being.) Indeed, it was unclear whether Choi was allowed to accompany his friend in the ambulance under the chaotic situation. Supposing Choi heard them accurately at whatever location, it was only logical to assume that they were articulated in English, as there was no report to the contrary.

For Vincent Chin to have uttered them as his last words, they gained an added dimension of import. Chin was adopted at an early age from Canton, China, by Lily Chan and her late husband. He appeared to have assimilated quite well and worked as a draftsman in Oak Park, Michigan. Seemingly another successful immigrant story, Chin most likely believed in the American sense of fair play: one worked hard to advance in a free, democratic, and just society. These words attributed to a dying Chin, therefore, were calculated to strike a chord with the American public, who were taught to believe in similar myths such as "rags to riches" and "equal under the law."

However, another string—if not the identical string—of words mumbled by Chin was heard by Officer Michael B. Gardenhire II, serving in his off-duty hours as a security guard at the McDonald's adjacent to the crime scene, who testified that Chin seemed to be conscious, lying in a pool of blood, and that Gardenhire could not understand what he was saying. In response to the government prosecutor Amy Hays's leading question, Gardenhire conceded that Chin could have been speaking in Chinese, which he would not have understood (*US v. RE*, No. 83-60629-CR, vol. 229, p. 90). At best a tangent in Hays's questions, this exchange on the witness stand nonetheless brought out an intriguing *perception*, one based on the assumption that a Chin adopted at the age of five from China retained Chinese to such an extent that his language before he went into a coma reverted back to his native tongue. Regardless of the validity of this perception, the prosecutor wished to stress Chin's foreign background in order to buttress the argument that the crime was racially motivated by whites against Asians. Both the alleged last words comprehended by Choi and those unintelligible ones assumed to be in Chinese represented various ways of inflecting the last moments of Chin's conscious life, which directly influenced the jury's and the public's view of the incident. Both approaches depicted Chin as a typical immigrant turned American, who died tragically at the hands of white racists.

The defense witnesses, perhaps instinctively, portrayed Chin in another stereotype of Asians — the combative kung fu master itching for a battle. Nitz asserted that Chin challenged them to continue the fight outside the bar as Chin was being escorted out. Chin was accused of deliberately taunting them: "Why don't you learn how to fight?" (*US v. RE,* No. 83-60629-CR, vol. 282, p. 104). By the same token, Starlene testified that she saw an Oriental man standing in "a martial arts stance" (*US v. RE,* No. 83-60629-CR, vol. 282, p. 41), waiting for someone down on the floor to get up. Even if Starlene were accurate in her account, her perception of "a martial arts stance" might have stemmed from her own stereotype of Orientals. In other words, when an Asian-looking person exhibited a readiness for physical engagement, it was likely to be interpreted as a menacing kung fu posture, particularly from an Oriental involved in a dispute with a choice client whom she allowed a short time earlier to "go down on her." The tragedy that befell Chin arose from Chin's "failure" to conform to the dominant stereotype of passive, effeminate Asian males.[7] He was so Americanized that he celebrated his upcoming wedding with a bachelor party at Fancy Pants, a public display of merriment and affluence deemed unacceptable from an Oriental. In addition, Chin was so macho that he threw the first punch in reaction to Ebens's verbal abuse. Both Nitz and Starlene drew from the stereotype of Asians as vengeful, bloodthirsty martial arts warriors popularized since the 1970s by Bruce Lee and the Hong Kong-Taiwan film industry. For obvious reasons, the defense suppressed the older stereotype of subservient, solicitous, yet often devious coolies (Ebens's reference to "boy" with its ring of black houseboys) in favor of the newer image of the aggressive fighter. To be sure, the newer stereotype does not cancel out the former. Rather, it builds on one particular strain of the old image, namely, the alien's inhuman cruelty.

A Riddle

The legacy of Vincent Chin sharpens the Asian American predicament: he was an American, but not to Americans; he was not an Asian, but he died as one.[8]

Part III
Multicultural Flaunting of Ethnicity

CHAPTER FIVE

The Chinese Siamese Cat
Chinoiserie and Ethnic Stereotypes

I was never able to precisely describe my discomfort with Amy Tan until I chanced upon her children's books — *The Moon Lady* (1992) and *The Chinese Siamese Cat* (1994), both illustrated by Gretchen Schields. Schields's graphics are an amalgamation of the style of chinoiserie, on the one hand, and of ethnic stereotypes of Chinese, on the other. Both sources for Schields's creation are Orientalized images of China. Chinoiserie idealizes Cathay, a mythic China; ethnic stereotypes demonize Chinese. The representation of China is hence polarized between two frozen moments — a timeless golden age of ritualistic festivity and a debased recent past of the Ching dynasty. The contradiction between the two Chinas recalls the coexistence of Charlie Chan, the good and entertaining detective, and Fu Manchu, the evil Oriental, in American popular culture. The West simplifies the other in stark black-and-white contrasts in order to situate itself squarely in the middle, resisting the evil heathens while aided by the loyal Asian servant. The female counterparts to the two archetypal males are the geisha Madame Butterfly, eager to please, and the Dragon Lady, eager to displease.

This chapter contends that Amy Tan partakes in the creation of a new, "alternative" Orientalism. To prove this, Schields's illustrations provide a starting point because the paintings embody what lies behind Tan's mass appeal. Tan is actually in an inextricable double bind. Having grown up in the 1960s when an ethnic consciousness movement permeated the United States, particularly her home city of San Francisco, Tan must have felt compelled to come to terms with the issue of ethnicity as an eminent Chinese American novelist since the instant sensation of *The Joy Luck Club* in 1989. But the roots-searching is equally informed and conditioned by the 1990s, where the urgency of racial identities slowly gave way to the exigencies of class interests.[1] Ethnicity in Amy Tan serves rather as a front for the psychological needs of her middle-class readers. Tan's racial essentialism, one based on a mystical landscape called China and a hidden yet indestructible Chinese bloodline, is articulated as a feel-good project for the writer and the reader, who wish to probe into ethnicity on paper, in fiction, so that real pains and afflictions in our midst can be averted. People of color as writers and as characters are welcome into American society, so long as they complement (or compliment) the mainstream culture. Indeed, with her well-assimilated, upwardly mobile, yuppie protagonists, Amy Tan is irresistible to devotees desperately seeking an alternative American myth.

Let me acknowledge at the outset that it would seem unfair to critique Tan the novelist solely on the basis of her books' illustrator. Tan clearly endorses her coworker's imaginings of China but is perhaps not responsible for Schields's use of chinoiserie and stereotypes. But what is at stake here is not a matter of legal accountability for, let's say, copyright disputes. Indeed, the personal relationship of the two partners is quite amiable. One cannot but suspect that the books carry more than Tan's blessings for joint business ventures. Schields appears to be a close friend of Tan's. *The Moon Lady* bears the dedication of "For our nieces with love," both Schields's and Tan's nieces. Tan includes her in the acknowledgments to all three of her novels, in addition to their cooperation to date on two children's books. Not only is Schields a confidant, but the subject matter of *The Chinese Siamese Cat* is close to Tan's heart as well. The book carries the dedication of "For Sagwa and Sluggo." Sagwa happens to be the name of the feline protagonist. Instead of a dedication to some fictitious characters, Sagwa (Sluggo as well?) is Tan's own pet cat, as the blurb to the hardcover edition of *The Hundred Secret Senses* (1995) states that Tan and her husband live in "San Francisco and New York with their cat, Sagwa, and their dog, Mr. Zo."

Even without such close ties to one's partner and subject, the "percentage" of culpability for the final product can seldom be conclusively determined between a writer and his or her illustrator. Art flows across the page from Tan's words to Schields's paintings and vice versa. Likewise, art permeates a young reader's mind as a holistic experience rather than disparately as written versus pictorial texts. To blame Schields alone for perpetuating Orientalism is to ignore the true reason for the very existence of the two children's books: the convergence of Tan's fame as a leading American writer of Chinese descent and of the Chinese subject matter of her children's books. Tan was already a commercially successful writer at the time of the publication of her first children's book. Although it may be Schields's fault that two seemingly contradictory images of China lie at the heart of the illustrations, the books sell more on the strength of Tan's reputation as an ethnic writer than on Schields's as an illustrator. The strange corollary seems to be that Schields's exotic China comes to be authenticated as China by Tan's reputation, which derives, to put it reductively, from her family name.

Let me also acknowledge at the outset that I may have disregarded the fantastic nature of the kind of children's literature to which Tan's work seems to belong. This line of argument would exonerate *The Chinese Siamese Cat* from a misrepresentation of reality on the basis of its alleged imaginary characteristics. Even fantasies, however, stem from perceptions of the outside world and in turn shape readers' perceptions of that world. In fact, no art is as neutral and detached from real life as some would have us believe. Like any other form of cultural expression, children's literature displays a particular relationship among the producers, the consumers, and the products.

Take, for example, Schields's twin inspirations, each of which came into being in the nexus of artistic expression, foreign market, and political and military might. Chinoiserie, a decorative art drawing from Chinese designs and images, flourished in Europe and England in the seventeenth and eighteenth centuries in the absence of Chinese art objects. The European demand for Chinese silk, porcelain, lacquer, furniture, and other wares propelled European artisans to create their own imitations of things Chinese. Anti-Chinese stereotypes, on the other hand, proliferated dramatically in the wake of European conquests over a weakened Ching dynasty since the 1830s. Colonialism is founded on the subjugation of other races, which must be conceptually justified through caricatures of inferior subjects.

But to the undiscerning eye, the material conditions and the historical precedents for Tan's children's books are irrelevant. Readers may not be concerned at all with the complex mediation from China to its representation. The authority of a single Chinese last name seems to collapse the several removes from China: the legacy of chinoiserie based on European taste for Cathay; the brutal political and economic system that called forth ethnic stereotypes; the fairy-tale nature of Amy Tan's children's books; the commercial interests dominated by the middle class, to name just a few.

Chinoiserie

Two book-length studies in English were devoted to chinoiserie. Hugh Honour's *Chinoiserie* was published in 1962, followed by Dawn Jacobson's book by the same title in 1993. The paucity of scholarship in this area is exemplified by how closely the two books resemble each other, as if no major development occurred during the intervening three decades. This reflects the attitude that chinoiserie is a minor art form, an attempt at reproduction of something authentic. In the postmodern era of simulacrum, chinoiserie merits another look, especially the political and cultural relationships it helps to illuminate. Both Honour and Jacobson adopt a historical approach with roughly the same periodization of chinoiserie; both texts use identical artworks as examples; certain passages from the two books are surprisingly similar. Both authors trace the genesis of chinoiserie to *The Travels of Marco Polo,* published in the early fourteenth century. Honour defines chinoiserie as "the expression of the European vision of Cathay" in the wake of Marco Polo (7–8). Jacobson likewise suggests that Polo's *Travels*

> presented a most tantalizing account of Cathay, as China was known to the medieval world, a land of wise government and elaborate courtesy, teeming with exotic natural phenomena and bursting with treasures. His book enshrined and distilled the fabulous vision of the East held by generations of Europeans, and played a starring role in the creation of chinoiserie, a style whose very being depended on an imperfect and romantic understanding of China. (13)

Such an "imperfect and romantic understanding" intensified during the Ming dynasty when the emperor banned foreign trade. The thirst for Chinese commodities created local imitations of Chinese porcelains and lacquers. The earliest extant imitations of lacquer were found in England in the first two decades of the seventeenth century (Honour 44). Interest in chinoiserie as a sign of opulence and elegance spread from the court to the city and then to other parts of Europe. Chinoiserie, as a consequence, is regarded by some as "fake" Chinese products.

Cultural influences, however, are hardly a one-way street. Cross-fertilization takes place even in the most imbalanced of power relationships (which is not to negate the reality of the relationships). Historically, while chinoiserie refers to European wares and textiles *à la Chine,* it does not exclude Chinese products made for export and hence made in accordance with European taste. Honour elucidates this through the example of eighteenth-century textiles: "Chinese weavers were producing fabrics adorned with the now famous 'tree of life' design, based on Indian patterns, derived from English originals which were an expression of the European vision of the Orient" (50). Therefore, it is ill-advised to treat chinoiserie as nothing but an artistic degradation of Chinese originals. Rather, this study is concerned with how the *ornamental* style of chinoiserie becomes equated with China, a China that exists as an *accessory* to the West. The way the preindustrialized Europeans manipulated the fabled Cathay suggests how Schields and, most important, Tan utilize the construct named China.

Anti-Chinese Stereotypes

All the "positive" imaginings of a culturally superior Cathay have frittered away since the 1830s. As Jacobson points out, "industrialization, commercialism and imperial interests [in Europe] all ran counter to the pinnacled fantasies of the chinoiserie style" (178). The crucial historical turning point in the Western attitude toward China occurred when Commissioner Lin Tse-hsu, charged with the enforcement of laws against the opium trade, burned in Canton the most lucrative cargo from British India to China. In response, England dispatched troops to capture Canton in 1840 and Nanking in 1842. The Treaty of Nanking ceded Hong Kong to England and opened four ports along China's coast. In 1860, the eighth Earl of Elgin led an expedition to capture Peking, raided the palaces, and burned the famed Yuan-ming-yuan, the garden to the imperial palace (Jacobson 182–83), ushering in an era that witnessed the decline of the Ching dynasty. To explain away the West's spoilage of a subcolonial China by means of repeated military operations and humiliating treaties, stereotypes emerged of a backward China populated by uncouth coolies with long queues, wispy literati with goatees and fans, corrupt, overweight, and long-nailed officials, and women with bound feet. All of these stereotypes are slant-eyed, some bucktoothed.

It is easier to describe what the anti-Chinese stereotypes are than to explain how they come about. Surely some Chinese, as well as some Westerners, exhibit these physical qualities, which are then indiscriminately imposed on all Chinese. The offensive slang word *slant,* for instance, refers to an Asian person. The perception of "slant-eyed" Chinese probably derives from the stylized facial features in traditional Chinese paintings, sculptures, and theatrical performances. Most characters in literati paintings from ancient China have the so-called *Feng-yen* ("Phoenix's eyes"). Performers in Peking Opera likewise practice *Tiao Feng-yen* whereby they pull the corners of their eyes upward and secure the stretched facial muscles with a headdress and tapes. But stereotypes in human relationships function in much the same way as chinoiserie did in cultural history. Certain external signs are ascribed to a group of people or artwork for the purpose of categorization and profit. Such ideological violence heralds, without fail, physical violence.

Gretchen Schields

The term *chinoiserie* as used in this chapter expands from a genre of art at a given moment in European history to an assembly of stylistic characteristics suggesting a particular perception of the Orient as a land of beauty and wisdom. At first blush, this utopian vision appears to jar against the ugly ethnic stereotypes. Yet the luxuriance and extravagance of Schields's illustrations intimate at the core of the Chinese universe a fundamental decadence, one prone to develop into negative traits. Sau-ling Cynthia Wong, in " 'Sugar Sisterhood': Situating the Amy Tan Phenomenon," coins the term "Oriental effect" on the basis of Roland Barthes's "the reality effect" to characterize Tan's "useless" details, whose existence is "allied with a kind of narrative *luxury* " and arises from a "discursive rather than referential" context (187–88). With regard to this children's book, both the written and the illustrated texts stem more from an Orientalist discourse than from the point of reference — China.

Schields's illustrations are filled with stock images of China: dragons, lions, goldfish, bats, magpies, birds in cages, decorative patterns, and, of course, human figures with stereotypical features. The most conspicuous affinity to chinoiserie is the decorative, fretted frames for each painting on facing pages (figure 25). The latticed edges can be in the traditional geometric shape, in the style of clouds, waves, arches, or

Sagwa was one of three pearl white kittens born to Mama Miao and Baba Miao, two fine cats who lived in a place everyone called the House of the Foolish Magistrate. The Foolish Magistrate was in charge of issuing rules and proclamations for the people and animals of his province.

If he had been a wise magistrate, he would have thought up rules to make others happy and healthy. A wise magistrate would have ordered people to care for cats who were sick or without homes. A *very* wise magistrate would have proclaimed that all cats should eat catfish every day.

But he was not wise. He made up rules that helped only himself. Because he wanted to command respect, he ordered people and animals to bow down to him. Because he was afraid people laughed at him behind his back, he made up a rule that people could no longer laugh. Because he wanted more money, he charged people fines for breaking his rules.

Figure 25. Amy Tan's *The Chinese Siamese Cat*. Reprinted with the permission of Simon & Schuster Books for Young Readers, an imprint of Simon & Schuster Children's Publishing Division, from *The Chinese Siamese Cat* by Amy Tan, illustrated by Gretchen Schields. Illustration copyright 1994 by Gretchen Schields.

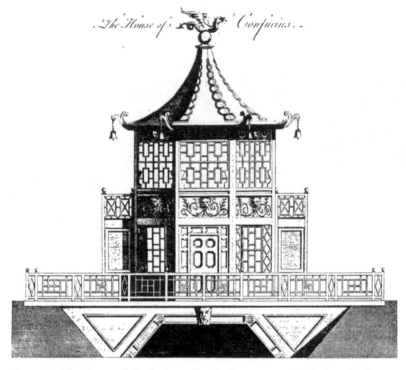

Figure 26. The House of Confucius at Kew, built ca. 1745 to the design of J. Goupy.

windows, or in a variation of all of the above. Chinoiserie has long inscribed fretwork as synonymous with things Chinese. A case in point is
the earliest recorded chinoiserie garden building in England, the House
of Confucius at Kew (figure 26), where latticework decorates the entire
building — railings, windows, doors, and even walls.

Such repeated, symmetrical, and often geometric designs are a style
decidedly favored by the Chinese throughout the centuries, but they
are hardly viewed by them as a signature *for* Chineseness. Indeed, human beings rarely take the initiative in reducing their multifarious selves
to a single surface trait. Such a paring down of complexities to "trademarks" that are readily identifiable is engaged in by others for conven-
ience and, ultimately, for control. A feature perceived by a "source" culture to be innate to itself is thus elected by the "target" culture as most
stylistically representative of the "source" culture. Both are, to be sure,
essentialist views. But it is one thing for Group A to perceive its members as slant-eyed and its architecture as filled with lattice-shaped dec-

oration. It is quite another matter for Group B to ascribe a distinct facial or architectural feature to Group A. Group A's self-perception may result from covert interpellation and overt indoctrination, but Group B's perception of others is blatantly oppressive.

Although a racial marker, the elaborately latticed frames act as windows to direct readers' attention to the center of the facing pages, where the story unfolds. In addition to the feline characters at the center, two groups of human characters are found, epitomized by the Magistrate and the Reader of Rules, on the one hand (figure 25), and the procession of singing and dancing figures, on the other (figure 27). The characters in figure 25 are all stereotypes. The Magistrate is absurdly overweight, pompous, and with knitted brows and long nails. He holds in his hand a pair of dragon-adorned opera glasses, a strange detail indeed. While spectacles imported from the West were rarities treasured by the elite during the Ching dynasty,[2] opera glasses were by no means so widespread as to justify outfitting the *only* bureaucrat and the symbol of authority with them. This intriguing detail exists less for historical accuracy than for evoking an association in the Western mind with upper-class women, privileged and fastidious, dangling opera glasses in their hands with long nails.

The Reader of Rules, who announces the Magistrate's harsh decrees, looks just as plain as all the other civilians kneeling before the Magistrate in figure 25, except that the Reader is more prominent in terms of his blue traditional dress and the stereotypical traits he exhibits. He wears a skullcap and a long queue (almost reaching the ground, as one finds out pages later). With a severe stoop, he sports a pair of round-rimmed, thick glasses. Similar to the opera glasses held by the Magistrate, there is a mysterious yellow pouch that hangs down from the Reader's shoulder. This pouch is noticeable whenever the Reader appears. One suspects that this is an allusion to tobacco (or opium?) pouches, as many Chinese smoked the pipe or the water pipe at the time. If indeed the pouch is implied to contain opium, Schields regrettably preserves a longstanding image of the depraved, opium-addicted Chinese. And of course, the eyes of all the Chinese characters slant, including those of the *Chinese* Siamese cats. The cats are given stereotypical Chinese features as well. Holding a fan, the male cat in figure 25 has goatees and slant eyes.[3] The fact that cats take on reputed Chinese characteristics is used by Tan and Schields to support the essentialism at the heart of the story: one's

They took to the streets with dogs barking and donkeys braying. They ran all the way to the Magistrate's house, singing at the top of their lungs.

Figure 27. Amy Tan's *The Chinese Siamese Cat*. Reprinted with the permission of Simon & Schuster Books for Young Readers, an imprint of Simon & Schuster Children's Publishing Division from *The Chinese Siamese Cat* by Amy Tan, illustrated by Gretchen Schields. Illustration copyright 1994 by Gretchen Schields.

ancestral bloodline determines one's identity, proven by the inherited physical traits of a race. But another conclusion can be drawn, namely, Chinese are (like) cats. This is a disturbing argument on the parallel of animals and humans in allegories and fairy tales best explored in the following section on Amy Tan.

In addition to cats as human beings in figure 25, there is a monkey garbed in human dress and standing upright, holding a parasol for the

Magistrate; evidently he is the Magistrate's attendant. Although the monkey myth is an integral part of Chinese civilization, exemplified by the powerful trickster Monkey in the sixteenth-century masterpiece *Hsi-yu-chi* (*Journey to the West*), there is scarcely any proof that in the Chinese iconography, high-ranking government officials and simian attendants are customarily juxtaposed. Chinoiserie, nonetheless, has the tradition of associating mandarins with monkeys. The most noted example is perhaps Christophe Huet's 1735 *grande singerie* in the Château de Chantilly, which displays "Chinamen" flanked by monkey servants (figure 28). Hugh Honour wrote that in the third decade of the eighteenth century, these simians began donning "flowing robes and assumed the airs of the mandarinate.... Whatever the origin of the cult [of *singerie*], monkeys came to be associated in the European mind with China before the end of the seventeenth century" (91). Honour and Jacobson were uncertain about the origin of *singerie,* but they seemed to agree on the centrality of the style of *singerie* enough to devote a section of their texts to it. Honour in fact titled his fifteen-page section "Monkeys and Mandarins in the France of Louis XV." Schields is borrowing not so much from a Chinese motif as from a chinoiserie construct of the Orient. The vexing implication of Chinese as animals, whether cats or monkeys, lingers.

Besides ethnic stereotypes, a second kind of human figure, one closely tied to the fantasy over Cathay, peoples Schields's illustrations. When celebration commences in figure 27, the procession of festivity consists of Peking Opera and Chinese folk art characters, whose costumes prove to be far more elaborate than the civilians' dress in figure 25 and hark back to a golden era seemingly beyond the flow of time. Their costume reminds one of *Nien-hua* (folk paintings for the New Year festival), an impression further reinforced by the dragon dance that is routinely performed during Chinese New Year. Celebrated with relatively stabilized symbols for generations, such as the dragon dance, new and colorful dress, and firecrackers, Chinese New Year becomes a ritual of mythic proportion, punctuating time yet transcending time. But the fact that Schields is evoking a festival so critical as to appear to be divorced from the routines of life does not give her the license to reinvent the tradition in the chinoiserie fashion. At the point when the Reader rushes to the people with the scroll of decree flying in the air to inform them of the new, altered proclamation, a wealthy man dressed as a *Yuan-wai*

Figure 28. *Singerie,* by Christophe Huet, ca. 1735.

(landlord) actually hugs a pig. The pig's nose ring, leash, and physical proximity to the *Yuan-wai* can only mean that the pig is a pet. With all the cluttered and historically verifiable, if somewhat stereotypical, details Schields gives of Chinese animals, this pet pig is truly out of place. If no evidence can be produced to prove that there was at one time the practice of raising pet pigs, then Schields undoubtedly paints in the school of chinoiserie that also spawned the likes of Mandarin and monkey.

As such, Schields's works are *not* about China but about what China is conceived to be by, and what China can be made to convey for, an American. But does "an American" include one with a Chinese face?

Amy Tan

The Chinese Siamese Cat follows Tan's typical narrative plot. A female Siamese cat tells a story to her brood of five kittens about their Chinese ancestry: a certain Sagwa "a thousand cat lives ago," whose blundering caused all Chinese cats to have "dark faces, ears, paws, and tails," despite the obvious migration from China to Siam or even to the West.[4] Sagwa, which should be "*Sagua*" based on the popular *pinyin* system of transcription, is the name of both the feline protagonist and Tan's pet cat to whom the book is dedicated. Tan explains in the story that Sagwa means "melon head" or "silly." While "silly" can be one of the definitions of Sagwa (meaning also "fool" or "idiot"), "melon head" is a bewildering rendering to any native speaker of Chinese. Wong, in " 'Sugar Sisterhood,' " has convincingly demonstrated that Tan's shaky grasp of the Chinese language comes to *fortify* a primarily female, white, middle-class following, who, in this instance, care less for the precision of translation than for the exotica of roman(tic)ized words. Similarly, Tan's fans — Wong calls them Tan's "sugar sisters," which derives from Tan's misreading of the address of respect "*Tang jie* " (female cousin) — casually dismiss the tremendous license the novelist takes in reconstructing Chinese life stories.

The remarkable discovery that a prominent Chinese American fiction writer would name her own pet "silly" and would erroneously take it to also mean "melon head" betrays how Tan is *at once* so close to, yet so remote from, her own ethnicity. Sagwa must be an object of love, much as Tan's Chinese heritage is close to her heart. However, she attributes to the name "Sagwa" as well as to her Chinese tales what is *not* there. With her fame founded on the exploration of Chinese materials,

Tan remains so ignorant of that culture as to commit egregious mistakes over and over again. Although endearing to her, Tan's China turns out to be highly imaginary and fabricated, like chinoiserie fashioned out of fragmentary images of Cathay, which nevertheless assuages the Western need for the other.

With a China plastic enough to suit her purposes, Tan's racial essentialism assumes that there exists a core of Chineseness passed down genetically, no matter how removed one is from one's origin. This internal "genetic signature," if you will, cannot be proven without its external manifestation. Thus the Chinese roots hinge on Siamese cats' shared features of "dark faces, ears, paws, and tails," around which Tan evolves her story. In addition to these physical characteristics, the retrieval of one's racial essence is graphically represented in terms of the cats' change of costume from the Western (not Siamese) to Chinese style, just at the moment the Siamese cat commences her story of Sagwa. All three of Tan's novels proceed along similar narratological contours: a beginning anchored in the consciousness of the thoroughly assimilated Asian American female protagonist, followed by the story of a life of adversity endured by her Chinese sidekick—the immigrant mothers in the first two novels and the half sister in *The Hundred Secret Senses*. For the sake of her young readers, Tan reduces the number of narrators in *The Chinese Siamese Cat*. Instead of the usual formula of opening the story with a "naive" Asian American and then switching to one who is older and capable of revealing the ethnic roots, Tan retains only the latter. Although Tan's texts supposedly depict communications between Chinese immigrants and their Chinese American relations, they are also a Chinese American storyteller's strategy for reaching her American readers in the 1990s in the name of—via the disguise of—one or several Chinese informants.

Oftentimes, these Chinese informants are given stories of themselves that most people of Chinese descent would hardly recognize. To illustrate, one revisits the protagonists of this story, Siamese cats. Siam (Thailand) and Japan were the only two Asian nations that successfully Westernized themselves in the nineteenth century; therefore, they escaped relatively unscathed from the fate of colonization befalling most of their Asian neighbors. The West's fascination with the East would occasionally spread from China and Japan to countries such as Siam, comparatively well known to the West. Siamese cats, because of their namesake, seem to be one of the stock associations of Asians in the Western mind, a representation any Asian in his or her right mind would hesitate to accept. That Tan should borrow such a degrading image as Siamese cats to embody her notion of Chineseness testifies to the fundamental dilemma in which she finds herself. To express her love for China, her as well as her readers' limited repertoire of things Asian forces the writer to adopt a stereotype based on caricature and racial discrimination.

To consider how Siamese cats have been summoned to entertain and educate the young in American popular culture (Tan is, after all, producing a children's book), I propose to turn to the quintessential American enterprise for youngsters: Walt Disney. Although demeaning racial vignettes are scattered throughout Disney productions, two feature-length animations stand out in the depictions of Siamese cats in what are purportedly Asian images. A bucktoothed Siamese cat in *The Aristocats* (1967) performs a "Chopsticks" song in "Ev'rybody Wants to Be a Cat." Using chopsticks to hit the piano keys, the cat sings in a flat, monosyllabic voice about alleged Chinese food such as Egg Fu Yung and fortune cookies from Hong Kong and Shanghai. The message in the fortune cookie is said to be never right; the semi-chant then ends with a silly snickering. It is revealing that both kinds of food are Western concoctions of Chinese cuisine, just as the portrayal of Siamese cats is meant for Western consumption.

By the same token, *Lady and the Tramp* (1955) features two wily, bucktoothed, cross- and slit-eyed Siamese cats disrupting the life of the canine protagonist, the "lady" of the title. The sound track to the cats' song is accompanied by dull monotones from percussion instruments (bells, drums, and tambourines), a parody of the monosyllabic Chinese language. The most biting burlesque comes through the lyrics, sung in the affected, high-pitched pidgin. The two cats repeat, in awkward, ungrammatical sentences, that they are Siamese whether or not it pleases others. If the accommodation proves satisfactory, chime the cats, they intend to stay put, which means serious disruptions of the lady's quiet life — alien intruders into a native lifestyle. These lines are dominated by the long "e" sound ("Siam*e*se" and "pl*ease*"), which arises from the assumption that the Chinese tend to end sentences with "e," such as the notoriously racist line "No tickee, no washee." The lyrics also suffer from unidiomatic expressions and a lack of *be*-verbs, all alleged characteristics of pidgin English. (It is far more effective to quote the exact lyrics of "Ev'rybody Wants to Be a Cat" and "We Are Siamese," where the racist characterization exposes itself, contrary to the G-rating, family entertainment image of Disney animations. But after having reviewed, among other things, the three pages before and after the page on which the lyrics appeared in my book manuscript, Disney denied my request for permission to reprint based on its "strict guidelines as to how our materials may be used" [letter from Disney, February 1, 2000].) Beyond such linguistic stereotypes, the cats' craftiness and duplicity surface in their scheme to eat the tropical fish and to steal the baby's milk. The refrain of the Siamese identity, furthermore, insists on an ethnic essentialism, one inherent in any use of stereotypes that posits genetically traceable physical, linguistic, and personality traits. Tan has taken up at least part of that tradition in her New Age ethnic drive. This is an entertaining comic scene for the insensitive but a terrifying one for those who are unfortunate enough to be identified as Siamese cats, in possession of such distorted attributes. The logic is frightening because, after all, pidgin English and such physical features are believed to be those of a certain group of humans. These alleged racial markers are transposed from humans to cats, not the other way around. Disney cats may then be regarded as projections of the Western perception of Asians.

To be fair to the executor of Tan's vision of felines, the Siamese cats are not as stereotypical and repulsive as Disney's. Although their eyes are slitty, bulging, and crossed, they at least do not have buckteeth. Although their faces are flat and with clumps of whiskers, they look rather adorable. No one suspects Tan and Schields of flagrantly perpetuating ethnic stereotypes as did Disney through the motif of Siamese cats. I would even suggest that Tan and Schields embarked on this joint venture out of good intentions toward Chinese and Chinese Americans. Herein lies the predicament for Asian Americans. For someone like Tan whose cultural arsenal in launching an oppositional discourse against Orientalism is circumscribed by her American identity, she is bound to duplicate Orientalist practices as often as she repudiates them. One may argue that I am guilty of presenting mere *circumstantial* evidence thus far in support of my assessment of Tan as a new Orientalist who collaborates in updating for our times the chinoiserie tradition and ethnic stereotypes of Chinese. I concede that perhaps nothing could convince die-hard Tan fans otherwise. But in case the readers are interested, they might, to rephrase the formulaic chapter closure in classic Chinese novels, turn to the next chapter, where I examine Tan's "alternative" Orientalism or New Age ethnicity in her most recent work, *The Hundred Secret Senses.*

CHAPTER SIX

"Chinese and Dogs" in
The Hundred Secret Senses
The Primitive à la New Age

New Age

Marianna Torgovnick's *Gone Primitive: Savage Intellects, Modern Lives* (1990) takes the pulse of the contemporary world in such a way that it sheds light on Amy Tan:

> [A]n essential fact of urban life in the last decades of the twentieth century: its polyglot, syncretic nature, its hodgepodge of the indigenous and imported, the native and the foreign. In the deflationary era of postmodernism, the primitive often frankly loses any particular identity and even its sense of being "out there"; it merges into a generalized, marketable thing—a grab-bag primitive in which urban and rural, modern and traditional Africa and South America and Asia and the Middle East merge into a common locale called the third world which exports garments and accessories, music, ideologies, and styles for Western, and especially urban Western, consumption. (37)

Reified and atomized in economies of advanced technology, the "Western" self feels drained, in need of recharging or healing in a spiritual sense, for which purpose the "primitive" Third World cultures are deployed. Simultaneously marked by its bestial savagery and spiritual transcendence, the primitive other is made to coalesce the physical with the metaphysical. In *The Hundred Secret Senses* (1995), imbued with such an ethos, the ethnic other's faculties of sight, hearing, taste, smell, and touch, as well as the capacity to feel, are intensified by fusions with animal senses and instincts in order to, paradoxically, invoke the hidden, essentialist, and extrasensory human soul. Tan's version of primitivism views rationality as an obstacle to the union of the body and the mind. To make sense of chaotic, damaged modern life, Tan routinely bypasses reason and descends to basic sensations, which, however, never take leave of the realm of nonsense entirely. Into this strange equation, Amy Tan interjects a third variable — ethnicity. Writing in the post-civil rights era, influenced by the multicultural milieu of the United States, Tan realigns the animalistic and the spiritual with the ethnic. The Chinese ancestry of her protagonists in *Secret* allows them to access the magical realm à la New Age, to be reborn as whole and wholesome human beings.

Tan's ethnicizing of the primitive contributes significantly to her success among white, middle-class, "mainstream" readers living in the climate of the New Age. As Torgovnick remarks in *Primitive Passions* (1997), "the New Age seems to be everywhere but continues to elude definition" (172). Resembling its hotbed of late capitalism, the New Age remains barely perceptible because of its omnivorous appetite of absorbing and commodifying alien cultural elements. That the New Age escapes precise definition should not, however, discourage us from contextualizing a writer such as Amy Tan in the New Age. Indeed, it is only through such a close reading of specific cultural practices that one comes to discern what has alarmingly been naturalized as a mode of life.

In consonance with consumerist social reality, Tan features San Francisco yuppies with New Age preoccupations with the self. Tan's breezy style is at its best as she depicts the protagonists, the Bishops, "busy" with their advertising business. Furthermore, the precise real estate lingoes of the Bishops during house hunting make possible the reader's identification with the protagonists through shared frustrations of the urban lifestyle. Interior decoration proves to be Olivia Bishop's forte as well. She expertly deciphers the layers of paint she removes from the wall of her newly purchased co-op: "a yuppie skin of Chardonnay-colored latex ... followed by flaky crusts of the preceding decades — eighties money green, seventies psychedelic orange, sixties hippie black, fifties baby pastels" (119). Olivia is the homeowner of, so to speak, the social history of the United States, a history that constructs the American identity.

With respect to the multicultural nature of this capitalist society, the mixed-blood Bishops embody the cultural hybridization of a minority such as Asian Americans. Tan's fascination with interracial characters predates *Secret* — for instance, Lena St. Clair in *The Joy Luck Club* (1989) and Jimmy Louie and his granddaughters, Tessa and Cleo, in *The Kitchen God's Wife* (1991). In *Secret*, the multiracial lineage crystallizes in Olivia's search for a proper last name on the eve of her divorce. She does not wish to revert back to her stepfather's name of Laguni, a fabricated Italian name for orphans. Nor does she want "Yee," the name and identity that Olivia's father usurps in order to come to the United States. "Bishop" is a name she intends to rid herself of but retains in the end. The ethnic impulse, nevertheless, is preserved as she names her newborn baby "Li" after her late half sister Kwan. Arguably, one can read in this obsessive whitening of characters throughout Tan's career a reflection of her assimilationism.

The portrayal of the yuppie's here and now entails, strangely, a New Age overreaching into the exotic/ethnic, or the "Chinese and dogs," as if the self would remain unfulfilled unless garbed in the primitive attire. It is important to note that the effort is not to efface the self but to embellish it. Wouter J. Hanegraaff has long asserted that New Age revisionism is a grab bag where "Oriental ideas and concepts have, almost without exception, been adopted only insofar as they could be assimilated into already-existing western frameworks" (*New Age Religion and Western Culture: Esotericism in the Mirror of Secular Thought* 517). Hanegraaff is echoed by Torgovnick, who finds New Agers to invariably put diverse rituals and symbols from other cultures "in the service of a thoroughly modern world view that takes the self as a thing to be owned, cultivated, and coddled — the veritable hub of the universe" (*Primitive Passions* 176), oblivious to the erasure of self in Buddhism and many other traditions.

Accordingly, Tan integrates the 1990s realism with Orientalist discourse. Tan's vivid, richly textured description of the lifestyle of the professional class, of their house-hunting saga, and even of the avalanche that threatens to demolish their life, contrasts sharply with the fuzziness of Changmian, China. The idyllic preindustrial countryside exists for the express purpose of touristic impressions and narcissistic wish fulfillment. The Bishops' "former life" or previous incarnation at Changmian during the Taiping Rebellion is similarly packaged in a set of tropes to ease the Western reader's entry into the Orient. American missionaries, Chinese bandits, and the Hakkas of the Taiping Rebellion led by the Christian convert Hong Xiuquan in the year of "*Yi-ba-liu-sì*" ("1864")

are arrayed to manage the alienness. And it is here that Tan's kinship
with the New Age ethos is blatantly exposed: she kneads together cultural elements as mutually exclusive as Christian linearity and Buddhist
cyclic reincarnation, or the 1990s yuppies and the 1860s Hakkas, to advance her plot.

Tan sets part of her story at the time of the Taiping Rebellion (1850–
64) during the Ching dynasty, a turmoil that exacts thirty million lives
and, according to Rudolf G. Wagner, is "the most important rebellion
of the nineteenth century" "with its decisive break with many traditional ideas such as footbinding, Confucianism, and its idea of selective
adoption of Western technology and institutions" (1–2). Wagner attributes the cause for this "best documented rebellion in Chinese imperial
history" to "the friendly contact sought by many missionaries and by
the Taipings themselves," resulting in "an usually large, if far from complete, body of original Taiping documents" (2). To suggest that the Taiping uprising is the "best documented rebellion" implies a Eurocentrism
whereby only source materials in Western languages seem to matter.
Amy Tan's interest is aroused, no doubt, by the abundant materials in
English and, in particular, by the role of the missionary in the event.

Moreover, the leader Hong Xiuquan was clearly influenced by the re-
vivalist tradition of "England and Scotland, the United States, Germany, and Sweden in the first decades of the last century" (Wagner 11).
The Taiping Rebellion was guided by Hong's vision obtained in his illness; Hong, in a state of delirious ecstasy, revealed that he was the
younger brother of Jesus, and son of God, mandated to eradicate the
devils of Manchus and Confucianism. Much of this history is extracted
by Tan, whose tale unfolds in the environs of the Thistle Mountain (Zi-
jing Shan), the Taiping stronghold in Guangxi (Robert P. Weller, *Resistance, Chaos and Control in China* 41).

In a similar vein, Tan borrows from the historical Hakka and the Buddhist notion of reincarnation. Hong Xiuquan and most of his followers
are Hakkanese. The feuding between the Hakka ("guest people") and
Punti ("local Cantonese") leads to the eruption of the Taiping Rebellion,
which serves to construct "Hakka identity through history" (Nicole Constable, *Christian Souls and Chinese Spirits: A Hakka Community in Hong
Kong* 29). Hakka's Christian belief, however fragmentary through Hong's
interpretation, assuredly contradicts the motif of reincarnation in *Se-*

cret. Progressing on a linear course toward heaven or eternal damnation, Christian theology is incompatible with the cyclic framework of Buddhism.

The heavy psychoanalytic bent of the New Age no doubt encourages Tan to view reincarnation in the Jungian sense as the accumulated result of karma or "psychic heredity." Tan's emplotment of karma at times betrays the casual attitude verging on unwitting mockery that New Agers take toward other traditions. The evil General Cape repays his debt to Miss Banner, Olivia's former self, by becoming Olivia's pet dog, hence neutralizing evil in a pseudo-Buddhist way. On the other hand, karma compels the interracial and cross-cultural Yiban ("Half-man") to be reborn as the mixed-race Simon Bishop. The adopted Elza instinctively reacts to Auschwitz because of her allegedly Polish Jewish ancestry. At the heart of Tan's arrogance in cosmic reshuffling of history and religion lies her affinity to the New Age movement.

Closely related to the 1960s counterculture, the New Age obsession with the self reflects the disillusionment with the sixties utopian vision, which "turn[ed] into the narcissitic Me Generation of the 1970s and the ambitious, self-involved young professionals of the 1980s...[Despite the apparent differences, they are children of the sixties in] the search for self-fulfillment in the here and now" (Dickstein 18). The title of Stephen A. Kent's essay crystallizes the evolution nicely: "Slogan Chanters to Mantra Chanters: A Deviance Analysis of Youth Religious Conversion in the Early 1970s." Tan in the 1990s continues the legacy of focusing narrowly on self-realization, even at the expense of coupling Chinese with dogs.

"Chinese and Dogs"

The celebration of Chineseness in Tan must be traced back to the Americanness of the author and her readers. The embrace of ethnic origin presupposes a source culture eager to be embraced, or one that is malleable enough for the author's fancy. This supposition leads Tan to conclude all three of her novels on the same note: the rediscovery of Chineseness beneath the protagonists' American veneer. Jing-mei June Woo's "Chinese genes" are felt to be activiated once her feet land on Chinese soil at the end of *The Joy Luck Club*. In *The Kitchen God's Wife*, Pearl's apprehension that she might be the daughter of the sadistic, demonic Wen Fu is dispelled by her mother, who weighs traditional Chinese principles of yin and yang over "genetics, blood type, paternity tests" (511), procedures that mark modern Western science. *Secret* likewise reveals the mixed-race Olivia coming to terms with her former life as a missionary in China. Beholding the beautiful landscape of Changmian, China, Olivia "feel[s] as if the membrane separating the two halves of my life has finally been shed" (205). For such a fantastic, potentially unflattering formula to strike a chord with "mainstream" American readers and create what Sau-ling Cynthia Wong calls the "Sugar Sisterhood" and the "Amy Tan Phenomenon," one suspects that Tan somehow validates the melting pot, the salad bowl, or a number of ethnocentric theories of American identity. Indeed, Tan's vision of multicultural America comes with trappings of Orientalism, upgraded by New Age chic, presented by hip San Francisco yuppies.

Tan's success hinges on her ability to revive Orientalist tropes as if she rejects them. To illustrate, one turns to the loaded phrase of "Chinese and dogs" in the context of nineteenth-century colonies like Hong Kong and foreign concessions. Imperialist history is enacted in Bruce Lee's *The Chinese Connection* (1972) when the sign outside a public park in Shanghai bars "Chinese and dogs" from entering. An outraged Lee then leaps into the air and kicks the sign to smithereens. The historical humiliation appears to metamorphose into an ethnic hubris in Tan since, initially at least, *only* "Chinese and dogs" gain entry into her New Age mystical fallacy. Following the modernist primitivism in the West, Tan celebrates the exotic Chinese other in the image of animals with supernatural instincts. Because the protagonists, Olivia and Simon Bishop, are both Amerasians, Western readers, by a strange but long-established Orientalist logic, could deduce that the noble savage is part of themselves as well. However, by no means is this part considered the core of the Western identity. In fact, that tie with primitivism can be shed like a piece of clothing, like the New Age guru Yanni's shifting sets of the Taj Mahal and the Forbidden City in a single telecast performance. By exploiting the thin line between the incomprehensible and the irrational, between the inspired and the insane, between the profound and the pathetic, between "secret senses" and nonsense, Tan is able to hold in double vision the comic Chinese sidekick Kwan, Olivia's half sister. Although endowed with mystical power, Kwan comes with the age-old baggage of Orientalism, evidenced in her pidgin English and her ludicrous ideas. At once a seer with "yin eyes" (3) and a specimen of superstitious gibberish, Kwan at one point of the novel attempts to explain "secret senses" to Olivia:

> "Ah! I already tell you so many time! You don't listen? Secret sense not really secret. We just call secret because everyone has, only forgotten. Same kind of sense like ant feet, elephant trunk, dog nose, cat whisker, whale ear, bat wing, clam shell, snake tongue, little hair on flower. Many things, but mix up together."
> "You mean instinct."
> "Stink? Maybe sometimes stinky—"
> "Not stink, *instinct*. It's a kind of knowledge you're born with. Like . . . well, like Bubba, the way he digs in the dirt."
> "Yes! Why you let dog do that! This not sense, just nonsense, mess up your flower pot!"
> "I was just making a—ah, forget it. What's a secret sense?"
> "How I can say? Memory, seeing, hearing, feeling, all come together, then you know something true in your heart." (102)

Tan bestows the human body with mysterious power. To draw from the resources available to all, Kwan tells the Secret that is the Body that is the Soul; or, the inner spirit accessed through human physical sensations equated with the animal's senses. The elaboration of the various animals' keenest sensory organs intends to bring out the magical nature of the secret sense. The choice of animal senses, however, exposes the author's scientific knowledge rather than Kwan's preindustrial training. Whereas "ant feet," "elephant trunk," "dog nose," "cat whisker," "bat wing," and "snake tongue" may be metaphors for mental sharpness in a number of old civilizations, "little hair on flower," "clam shell," and "whale ear" are pieces of information most likely accrued by students of modern science. It is fairly difficult to envision a Kwan sitting through PBS's *Nature* or *Nova* to obtain scientific knowledge. At least, the novel does not depict such scenes.

Nevertheless, the refrain of animal senses proceeds in pidgin English, entirely without the proper possessive unit, hence achieving a nonsensical quality to it, one that recalls Charlie Chan's aphorisms. Despite Kwan's seemingly random speech pattern, Tan uses pidgin English with great precision and calculation, illustrated by the wordplay on "stink" and "*instinct*" (italicized in the original). Further borrowing from Orientalist practices lies in Olivia's frustration with Kwan's explanation of secret senses, a frustration that echoes the reader's inability to understand Kwan. Olivia's "I was just making a—ah, forget it" eerily resembles the concluding line of Roman Polanski's *Chinatown* (1974): "Forget it, Jake! It's Chinatown!" Chinatown comes to exemplify the evil and unjust world, totally beyond human comprehension; the private detective played by Jack Nicholson is therefore urged to forgo the pursuit of criminals in or outside of Chinatown.

The deliberate pidginization of Kwan's dialogue comes into sharp focus when, half a dozen pages later, Tan has Olivia retell the same animal kinship with secret senses. During Kwan's seance with Simon's late girlfriend, Elza, Olivia believes that she in fact feels Elza's spirit:

> [Elza] wasn't like the ghosts I saw in my childhood. She was a billion sparks containing every thought and emotion she'd ever had. She was a cyclone of static, dancing around the room, pleading with Simon to hear her. I knew all this with my one hundred secret senses. With a snake's tongue, I felt the heat of her desire to be seen. With the wing of a bat, I knew where she fluttered, hovering near Simon, avoiding me. With my tingly skin, I felt every tear she wept as a lightning bolt against my heart. With the single hair of a flower, I felt her tremble, as she waited for Simon to hear her. Except I was the one who heard her — not with my ears but with the tingly spot on top of my brain, where you know something is true but still you don't want to believe it. (107)

A strategic retreat from Kwan's exclusively animal imageries, Olivia marshals New Age electromagnetic, biochemical terminologies. The ghost becomes gyrating "sparks," "a cyclone of static, dancing around the room." Olivia's pseudoscientific language dimishes the distance of the protagonist from the middle-class reader, from whom Kwan's jabbering serves only to alienate. Even when the same kind of elemental, primordial references to animal senses are raised, they are accomplished through parallelism and in perfect English, with the proper grammatical structure restored: "a snake's tongue," "the wing of a bat," "my tingly skin," and "the single hair of a flower." Olivia's "translation" of Kwan's remarks is crucial to link the ethnic other with the modern reader. The reinterpretation helps sustain the tension between Oriental stupidity and mystery.

Granted, this shift from pidgin to standard English seems justified by the two speakers' varying proficiencies of the English language. And Tan has indeed matured stylistically in *Secret* by eschewing the artificial divisions between four pairs of mothers and daughters in *Joy* and the privileging of the mother's Chinese tales in *Kitchen*. In her third novel,

Tan has learned to do three different voices exceptionally well and, moreover, to interweave them seamlessly: the hip, fluent English of the American-born Bishops; the simple, stilted English taken to be literal translation of Kwan's stories in Chinese; and Kwan's pidgin, which mangles English for comical effect. Besides, to attribute Kwan's pidgin to her nonnative-speaker status obfuscates the crux of the problem: the novelist's white gaze at Kwan. Tan inscribes Kwan with a linguistic exoticism that could only stem from an outsider's ears, a fact painfully clear if one compares Kwan's English with Louis Chu's language in *Eat a Bowl of Tea* (1961). Representing the ghettoized community in postwar Chinatown, Chu develops a vulgar, abusive, and vivid language that befits the disgruntled bachelors. The Chinese men endlessly exchange insults, such as "many-mouthed bird, go sell your ass"; "you dead boy"; "shut up your mouth" (not simply "shut up"); "wow your mother"; "where are you going to die?" Marlon K. Hom in his review of the novel commends Chu for translating "the Chinese speech faithfully into lively English" and for "retain[ing] the source language's original figurative and picturesque idiomatic expression." Chu accomplishes this because he takes an insider's position vis-à-vis his characters' dialogues, eschewing "the literal translation of Chinese speech into the servile, stilted English" or a transliteration of "Chinese sounds" followed by "appended English explanations" (98). However, the subtleties of Chu's conversations—for example, "shut up your mouth"—would only be captured by a bilingual reader. To an English-speaking reader, Chu's language seems far less inviting than Kwan's fortune cookie "spitch," to borrow from Frank Chin's phrase in *The Year of the Dragon*.

In addition to meshing together the three Englishes (fluent, stilted, and pidgin), Tan even attends to the possibility of a fourth linguistic scenario: the failure of Olivia's English in China. On the airplane to China, an Olivia paranoid about crashes does not know how to order, in Chinese, "gin and tonic" to calm her nerves. And Kwan seems to take special delight in Olivia's difficulty. Olivia once again comes up short when she tries to win over a cowherd who, having heard her tense and lengthy explanation, replies "in perfectly enunciated English," "Assholes" (294). That cowherd turns out to be another Asian American tourist.[1] With this episode, Tan exhibits her grasp of the changing demographics of Asian Americans and the forces of globalization. In view of her meticulous depiction of the multiplicity of Asian American subjectivity, it becomes even more disconcerting to see how she clings to nineteenth-century stereotypes of the Orient and the Oriental, albeit with a New Age twist.

Put bluntly, Kwan the Chinese "familiar" is a dog, serving doggedly the Chinese American master, Olivia. Kwan's "doggedness" comes through in the determined pursuit of Olivia through reincarnations, in the loyalty to and solicitations of Olivia, despite utter humiliation, and in her obtuseness, one is forced to conclude from her bad English and superstitions. Ever since her debut in the narrative, Kwan is in fact accompanied by animals and insects. Upon her arrival in the United States, Kwan offers Olivia a gift of a grasshopper, which sends Olivia bawling in the airport. Tan adopts the microscopic, anatomical description of the cricket to demonstrate the alienation and instinctive rejection Olivia feels toward Kwan, her newly arrived Chinese past. A common plaything for Chinese children, the grasshopper is defamiliarized as "a six-legged monster, fresh-grass green, with saw-blade jaws, bulging eyes, and whips for eyebrows" (10) a description fraught with monosyllabic, pseudo-Chinese sounds. Once again, the first thing Kwan undertakes upon return to China is to release a snow owl. The strategy of defamiliarization continues to function in that the owl is originally destined for the Chinese dining table, a barbaric practice to the affluent First World. Not just Kwan but all Chinese are animal-related. Miss Banner, Olivia's previous incarnation, calls her Hakka companion, Kwan's former self, "Miss Moo," after the sound of a cow.

The proximity to animals highlights the keen senses of the Chinese and sinophile characters. Miss Moo "felt a twist in my stomach, a burning in my chest, an ache in my bones" (174), in the wake of Miss Banner's elopement with General Cape and hence abandonment of her friends. The elopement may well be brought about by, Miss Moo regrets, her own praying for Miss Banner's happiness, a terrible irony that "shriveled my [Miss Moo's] scalp" (63). Searing human feelings of these characters are often narrated in awkward English to achieve an Orientalist effect, to defamiliarize universal emotions as exotic, somehow deeper, ones. Describing Miss Banner's misfortune, Miss Moo says that "she grew many kinds of sadness in her heart" (47), an unidiomatic and somewhat poetic expression that suggests at once foreignness and aestheticism. Note that Miss Moo's refrains of the body, be it "stomach," "chest," "bones," "scalp," or "heart," bring forth the physical coordinate in the New Age attempt at spiritual healing. Tan uses these deep pains in sensory terms as springboards for extrasensory or trans-material leaps across the "karmic circle" (91).

The call of the primordial/spiritual is so strong that even the interracial yuppie Olivia cannot ignore it. In other words, Olivia's body "doggedly" feels the pull of her former life in China, just as her Americanized mind dismisses it. Whenever traumatic events in her life flash through the story, Olivia resorts to pidgin identical to Miss Moo's or Kwan's: the memory of electroshock treatments administered on Kwan "hurt my [Olivia's] teeth" (16). Olivia's dreams based on her violent death at the hands of the Ching dynasty soldiers are saturated with sensory impressions: "I've tasted cold ash falling"; "I've seen a thousand spears flashing like flames"; "I've touched the tiny grains of a stone wall"; "I've smelled my own musky fear"; and so forth. Such impressionistic snippets echo other intense moments in Olivia's life, such as the witnessing of Elza's ghost and the book's finale in the valley of the soul when Olivia smells the "dank, fusty odor... an olfactory version of déjà vu — déjà senti... like the way animals know" (310).

Before the knowing arrives, however, un-knowing or the un-learning of rationality has to occur. In the exotic China, presumably their place of origin, Olivia and, to a lesser degree, Simon abandon control and become the Chinese other that is, in Tan's logic, the "essence" of the self. The key moment for this identity transformation comes while Olivia photographs the almost ritualistic killing of a chicken for a feast welcoming her and other American guests (264). Olivia acts simultaneously as an ethnographer documenting some primitive initiation rite and as an accomplice "shooting" the chicken whose blood is slowly being drained. Unlike Simon who passes judgment ("That was fucking barbaric. I don't know how you could keep shooting" [264]), Olivia submits herself to China, "where I have no control, where everything is unpredictable, totally insane" (261), leading her "instincts [to] take over" for photography. Tan, however, tries to deflate this sublime instant in the same way that Kwan's prophecy sounds also like idiocy. When Olivia inquires after the procedure of the killing, the old woman responds that she prolongs the chicken's death throes "for your photos" (265).

Subsequently, Olivia and Simon join in the uncivilized and hence the supracivilized as they follow the lead of Kwan "at a half-crouch" to squat around to partake of the chicken dinner (266). With such postures increasingly found only in the Third World, they plunge deeper into the land of oblivion by consuming the local brew, "pickle-mouse wine.... Very famous in Guilin."[2] At the bottom of the wine bottle lurks "something gray. With a tail." In response, the Bishops' brains tell them to "retch," but they burst out "laughing" instead (268). Guilin itself does not produce any world-renowned liquor, whereas the province of Guizhou adjacent to Guilin geographically and close in pronunciation boasts of the wine of mao-tai. Mao-tai, of course, bears no resemblance at all to the sensational "pickle-mouse." It is fairly difficult to conceive of the Chinese, including the Hakkanese who are alleged to inhabit Changmian, naming their wine after a mouse, a pest as much detested in China as it is in the West. Even though the local characters may have concocted the name to poke fun at the Bishops, the ultimate creator of the phrase is Amy Tan. Revealingly, Tan's brand of spirits is christened in accordance with her New Age primitivism. With the function of "brain[s]" or reason suspended, a revolting sight turns into the threshold of an epiphany.

In the same breath as the misnaming of wine, Tan misinterprets the site of the story as well. The fabricated site of Changmian is taken to pun, in Mandarin, both "sing silk" and "long sleep." Equally poetic, both translations of the village name accentuate the gist of the novel. The protagonist Olivia's past life and the buried mementos in Changmian are to be excavated in this present life by means of her secret senses, windows to one's soul. The two halves of the self are separated and linked, metaphorically, by a long hibernation in the image of Hakka's "neverending" folk songs like silky threads. However, "mian" means "cotton" rather than "silk" (275). It may not simply be Tan's inadequate understanding of the Chinese language that results in this error. Tan is likely to be romanticizing the Orient in the stock images of silk, jade, porcelain, and so forth, whereas cotton readily evokes the American South and slavery, associations entirely inappropriate in the context. Granted that "silky" is more romantic than "cotton-like," granted that "picklemouse" is more revolting than the meaningless mao-tai, Tan's consistent mismanagement of the Chinese language and culture is calculated to bring forth a fictional universe at once aesthetic and abominable, at once uplifting and degrading, in the exact Orientalist formula.

Initiated by ritual killing and sharing, of Bacchus-like intoxication, this dislocation of the Bishops' reasoning faculty is helped along by the renaming of objects and places. So is the whole elaborate scheme of the

Bishops' homecoming across continents and reincarnations. Put another way, the Bishops' previous lives as unrequited lovers in mid-nineteenth-century China serves principally to silhouette their present crisis in marriage and to provide the means for a happy resolution. As such, the ceremony of wine and food concludes on a marriage bed. The inebriated couple makes love on a traditional marriage bed, after months of separation. Willfully and unabashedly, Tan manipulates the representation of the other for her own ends; Tan's New Age appeal lies ultimately in such facile usage of the primitive other. A marital dilemma or identity crisis that modern readers readily identify with is resolved in a revisiting of some magical fountain of youth, which blends animalistic, spiritual, and ethnic components.

The New Age obsession of healing never fails to loom behind the trope of China. Each and every one of Tan's female characters suffers from one illness or another. The Chinese matrons are often so strong-willed and "negative-thinking" (*Kitchen* 152; as opposed to the New Age precursor of "positive thinking") that they are taken to be mentally unstable, their malaise deriving from excessive repression of the past. The Chinese American daughters are likewise caught in the emotional quandary of loving and hating their mothers. Tan's women are constantly plagued by the loss of their children, siblings, or parents. Specifically in *Kitchen*, the protagonist Pearl is afflicted with multiple sclerosis, Aunt Helen with a brain tumor, and Pearl's mother with too much pain and abuse from her first husband.

More appallingly, doglike Chinese companions often have to be sacrificed in this spiritual convalescence for Chinese Americans. At the end of *Secret*, Kwan vanishes into Changmian's labyrinth of caves in exchange for, in a manner of speaking, Simon's return. The bittersweet, melodramatic reunion of the Bishops entails Kwan's disappearance. Of course, the melodramatic plot culminates in the birth of the Bishops' Samantha Li, who is given Kwan's last name in part because she is supposed to be Kwan's reincarnation. As James Moy diagnoses in "The Death of Asia on the American Field of Representation," "only through its [Asia's] death, or representational self-effacement, does Asia become real for Western audiences" (356). "Real" in the sense of "functional" or an irreplaceable ingredient in the Orientalist discourse, Kwan is preceded by Giocomo Puccini's Madame Butterfly and, in Tan's *Joy*, by Suyuan Woo, Jing-mei June Woo's mother, who dies to make possible the emotional return to

China of the American-born June. To a lesser extent, Grand Auntie Du in *Kitchen* dies in the opening chapter to pave the way for the protagonists' disclosures of their secrets. Tan's melodrama of ethnicity hinges on the coexistence of tragic demise of the Chinese characters and rebirth of the Chinese American ones. One cannot help recalling the episode in Tan's *Kitchen* revolving around the Shanghai prostitute Min. Min performs masochistic illusions of being tortured to death for the entertainment of mostly foreign clientele at Shanghai's Great World in the French concession. While the author purports to criticize foreign encroachment of China via Min's torn limbs, it is ironic that Tan's imagination invariably involves the death of Chinese sidekicks for the recovery or self-discovery of Chinese American protagonists.

In closing, I find it hard to resist a silly wordplay: "dog" spelled backwards becomes "god."[3] To Amy Tan, "Chinese dogs" and "Chinese gods" are one and the same, dogs deified, gods mongrelized. With both qualities instilled into "Chineseness," Tan's true motive is the construction of the American self that engineers and marionettes New Age ethnicity and primitivism. By rendering the Chinese simultaneously animalistic and divine, Tan in effect becomes an invisible creator, whose creatures reenact the Orientalist fantasies of her massive "mainstream" following.

CHAPTER SEVEN

Mulan Disney, It's Like, Re-Orients

Consuming China and Animating Teen Dreams

The Name of the Dish

As Chinese legends have it, Mu Lan's family name is Hua, or, in Maxine Hong Kingston's Cantonese version, Fa. Inspired most likely by her *The Woman Warrior* (1976), the 1998 Disney animation *Mulan* calls the protagonist "Fa" as well. But in the film, she largely goes by her first name, while called "Ping" during her cross-dressing disguise. The rendering of her given name, Mulan, in the pinyin system, thus ridding it of the more defamiliarizing space and capitalization, makes possible easy identification between the young audience and the protagonist with an English-sounding name. Lest I be found a carping critic on the point of Mulan's spelling, one must realize that Mulan, along with the dragon-lizard Mushu, are in fact exceptions to the rule of Chinese-sounding names; they are outnumbered, based on Disney's accompanying children's book, by Fa Zhou her father, Fa Li her mother, Shan-Yu the Hun chieftain, Chien-Po the bald giant, Cri-Kee her familiar, and others. The splitting of the word "cricket" to create the monosyllabic "Cri-Kee" demonstrates the Orientalist context within which Mulan's more English-sounding name appears. Indeed, the overwhelming majority of characters have names that are, at once, exotic and familiar — the precise Orientalist formula of projecting the self's deepest longings onto the other, a magic mirror dwarfing and caricaturing none other than the self taken to be someone else. The yoking of strangeness and banality in Orientalist representations succeeds in accommodating and domesticating the unknown. Hence, Mulan's steed is "Khan," after Genghis Khan. Her com-

panion, the dragon-lizard, is Mushu, after Mooshu Pork. Her masculine disguise is called Ping, after an imperial court mandarin in Puccini's
Turandot (1926).

Mulan's hidden last name, however, is Disney. Mulan Disney now joins
the lineage of animated female characters, all of them with suppressed
surnames — Snow White, Cinderella, Sleeping Beauty, Jasmine in *Aladdin,* Pocahontas, Belle the Beauty, and others. Although endowed with
various cultural and national identities, they are all, by blood, children
of Disney. Reflecting the desires of the multicultural, Gen-X (-Z?) audience in the United States, these characters are composites based on
images, stereotypes, and fantasies of the other. With respect to images
of Asians in the 1990s productions, they are no longer blatantly racist,
like the sly, bucktoothed, cross- and slit-eyed, and pidgin-speaking
Siamese cats in *Lady and the Tramp* (1955) and in *The Aristocats* (1967).
Having said that, one hastens to add that Mulan and her nineties' siblings, born out of multiculturalism, serve to manage, within the United
States and elsewhere, the drastically changing demographics and the
concomitant conflicts of cultures; the Disney bunch not only entertains
but brings into conformity with the adolescent American sensibility
an alienating and occasionally hostile world. Just as the global village is
becoming complex daily, Disney offers simplistic visions of the exotic
other — China — to allay the audience's fear. In an effort to re-orient (pun
intended), rather than dis-orient, *Mulan* supplements Orientalist fantasies with contemporary youth culture. The waves of laughter during
a screening of *Mulan* are perhaps expressions of children's innocence,
cheering them up before the long journey into William Blake's experience.

Unlike Sean Connery's *The Name of the Rose* (1986), where the poetic title belies a film that has nothing to do with roses, the subhead for
this section, "The Name of the Dish," points straight to the problematics of *Mulan.* The dish Mooshu Pork brings into being the character
Mushu, in an unmistakable association with Chinese cuisine. Mushu's
concluding line of the film is "Call out for egg rolls!" for the dancing
party of Fa Mulan's ancestors in celebration of her triumphant return.
Whether Chinese takeout, appetizer, or entrée, the fetish of Chinese food
has so interpellated the Western consciousness that Disney never both-
ers to capitalize on Mushu's origin, as it were, until the last line of the
film. However, Mooshu Pork is a corruption from the standard yet nearly
unpronounceable spelling of, in Wade-Giles, "Mu Hsu" or, in pinyin,

"Muxu." Moreover, the second vowel in Mooshu should be "ü." Clearly a long-standing compromise with English-speaking customers, the entrée has always been listed on the menu as Mooshu Pork. After all, one is not likely to order a dish one cannot vocalize. The seeming chaos of an Orientalist culinary universe to many Westerners must be commanded linguistically ("Let there be — Mooshu!") before it can be consumed.

Consuming China

In *Mulan,* the sensory consumption of China is predicated on the abundance of iconography of the Orient, which can be divided into three categories: animate icons, inanimate icons, and human relationships. Animate icons in *Mulan* consist of animals and insects, of which the Magic Kingdom boasts a long tradition. The protagonists of *Mulan* are almost always accompanied by nonhuman familiars, such as Mulan's puppy, the black horse Khan, the dragon-lizard Mushu, and the cricket. Although playing second fiddle to Mulan, these familiars are instrumental in moving the plot, in generating fun, and in Orientalizing this Disney product for consumption.

The diminutive dragon-lizard Mushu, demoted for past offenses, is dubbed by the African American actor Eddie Murphy, whose jokes stem largely from the streetwise black lingo. Mushu's lines gush out with dizzying speed, which befits the MTV pace of the film and the short attention span of a young audience. When subjected to prolonged contemplation, however, Murphy's performance reveals its schizophrenic nature. Murphy has always been a chameleon of a comic, changing himself into a host of black characters with entirely different physical and speech traits. Makeup artists worked wonders on Murphy in *Coming to America* (1988), in which he triples as a barber, a singer, and a Jew, in addition to an African prince. Murphy once again doubles as an obese scientist and a playboy in *The Nutty Professor* (1996). The only role transgressing racial lines is Murphy doing an elderly Jewish man with a stereotypical Jewish nose and a strong East European accent at a barbershop in *Coming to America*. A response to blackface performances from Al Jolson to Gene Wilder in *The Silver Streak* (1976), the talented Murphy pays back in kind. Having previously striven to impersonate another race — the Jew — Murphy-Mushu is unadulteratedly black. Whereas the Jewish Murphy impresses through how thoroughly he sheds his blackness, the Chinese Murphy wears race like the emperor's new clothes, unabashedly exposing an ebony self. Perhaps Murphy has no choice: the Jew speaks with a heavy accent, but not one that crosses over into racist caricature; it would have been inexcusable, however, had he adopted the singsong Chinese pidgin for Mushu's dialogues.

It is tempting to attribute the difference of Murphy's Jewish and Chinese personae to the diverging demands of live-action films and animations. Realism has come to dictate Hollywood dramas. Hence, to perform a particular race, one has to be like that race, or at least to take on the outer trappings and stereotypical images of that race. Any mismatch between physical traits and dialogues defeats the realistic facade. Animations are make-believe, supposedly free from the bondage of the real and the factual. Dubbing for animations, furthermore, entails the paradox of a voice *divorced from* the body and yet *belonging to* the body. Although filmically the audience does not see Murphy, it knows that it is he, particularly when Disney's advertising campaigns never fail to include the names of the Hollywood stars who lend their voices to its animations.

The difference between live-action drama and animation aside, however, the alarming fact remains that Murphy expends no effort to acquire any semblance of Chineseness, whatever that means linguistically. Supposedly performing in yellowface, there is simply no pretense as to his blackness. One of the multicultural ploys (plays) of the 1990s Disney productions, Mushu juxtaposes irreconcilable ethnic elements of Orientalist appearance and black English, as if racial differences could be resolved accordingly. The other extreme of Disney's dubbing practices is the racial essentialism in having prominent Asian American performers do Chinese characters: Ming-na Wen for Mulan, B. D. Wong for Shang, Noriyuki Pat Morita for the Chinese emperor. Disney's facile approach to multiculturalism is a wish fulfillment, deriving from and hence validating racial stereotypes. The transparency of race inherent in Murphy's inner-city black dialect bespeaks the relative powerlessness of the Asian American constituency; Disney takes this calculated risk of offending a particular minority for the potential profit it might garner from the majority and other minority groups.

In terms of Orientalist appearance, Mushu is the caricature of the dragon, the trite trope for China, equipped with long strands of goatees. Almost all the major characters, it goes without saying, sport "proper" Orientalist markers — slant eyes, round moon faces, long straight hair, and goatees for males. In addition to her steed Khan and her dragon guardian Mushu, a cricket accompanies Mulan as well. Notwithstanding the precursor of Jiminy Cricket in *Pinocchio* (1941), the choice of a cricket in the cast accentuates the limited repertoire of Orientalism, resorted to by Westerners whenever the need to represent China arises. In *The Last Emperor* (1988), the first film ever made by a Westerner inside China after the Cultural Revolution, Bertolucci features a grandiose scene at the Forbidden City where Pu Yi—the last emperor of the Ching dynasty—is inaugurated. Amid hundreds of kowtowing officials, the young emperor is hooked by the sound of a cricket and eventually discovers its whereabouts. After a lifetime of impotence, corruption, and suffering, the gardener Pu Yi in the People's Republic of China returns at the end of the film to visit the Forbidden City, where he retrieves, miraculously, the cricket cage hidden behind the throne. While allegedly making a historical film of epic proportion, Bertolucci sees fit to integrate magical touches via a cricket to highlight Pu Yi's childlike innocence. The Chinese American novelist Amy Tan, likewise, introduces a grasshopper alongside Kwan in *The Hundred Secret Senses* (1995). The cricket in *Mulan* is made to symbolize good luck, and much amusement stems from how Cri-Kee fails its task.

The iconography of China includes as well props or inanimate icons. The film opens with the Great Wall and ends with the Forbidden City.[1] In between the well-known historic sites, tired Orientalist objects are repeatedly deployed: dragon flag which Shan-Yu burns on the Great Wall, dragon statue in Mulan's family garden, dragon wall covering in the emperor's palace, dragon cannons that annihilate Shan-Yu's army, dragon dance concealing Shan-Yu's henchmen, dragon pendant bestowed upon Mulan by the emperor. Besides dragons, plum blossoms decorate a classical Chinese garden where a traditional scene of filial piety between Mulan and her disabled father unfolds. No films on ancient China are complete without some kung fu sequence. As such, the commander Shang, later Mulan's intended, trains the new recruits in martial arts. The final showdown between Mulan and Shan-Yu takes place on the grounds of the Forbidden City, embellished with traditional Chinese lanterns and fireworks. Other seemingly authentic details of China abound, such as Mulan's hair comb, chopsticks, and ink brush. Mulan eats with chopsticks but no Chinese would be so ill-mannered as to thrust the chopsticks upright in the rice bowl. No rice bowls, for that matter, would pile up like a mound. She writes with a brush, but her calligraphy winds up on her wrist.

Finally, human relationships are constructed in accordance with clichéd notions of the East. Mulan attempts to bring "honor" to her family by attending the bride selection, which proceeds, incidentally, with monotonal music and monosyllabic lyrics. Another manifestation of the constricted repertoire of Orientalism, Disney's foregrounding of "honor" harks back to Puccini's *Madame Butterfly,* where the Japanese geisha commits ritual suicide upon discovering her shame and dishonor. Similar to Amy Tan's rehashing of the trope of grasshopper in *The Hundred Secret Senses,* David Henry Hwang, in his self-styled "deconstructivist" *M. Butterfly* (1988), borrows as his recurring motif Puccini's line "Death with honor / Is better than life / Life with dishonor" (15). Both of Chinese extraction, Tan and Hwang are so deeply immersed in Western culture that their respective attempts to subvert Western hegemony ends up perpetuating that hegemony.

Failing to "honor" her family through marriage, Mulan subsequently embodies "filial piety" in substituting for her ailing father in battle. Disney, however, overdoes the Orientalized social customs in presenting an exposed Mulan on the verge of being beheaded. As the military counsel makes clear, tradition decrees capital punishment for the offense of cross-dressing. Neither the folk legend of Hua Mu Lan nor the extant "Ballad of Mulan," written anonymously during the sixth century A.D., depicts this crisis. If anything, "The Ballad of Mulan" offers an almost uneventful transformation from her male disguise back to femininity. "Just lend me a fleet-footed camel / To send me back to my village," requests Mulan of the emperor. "When my parents heard I was coming, / They helped each other to the edge of town" (Liu and Lo 79). What is missing in the translation is the gender-specific references: "send me back to my village" should be "send boy [son] back," and "When my parents heard I was coming" should be "When my parents heard girl [daughter] was coming." The awkward literal renditions hope to bring out the gender switch as Mulan moves from her public role in the presence of the emperor to her private self in the family. The social context entails a gender switch.

Disney, on the other hand, is more concerned with creating suspense to hold the audience's attention. Surely a boost to the dramatic tension when Mulan is saved only by Shang's love and hence his countermanding of so-called tradition, the sword lifted above Mulan's neck neverthe-less sharpens the perception of a misogynist Orient where, in Maxine Hong Kingston's memorable words, girls are "maggots" and "worse than geese." Other than the sexist mores, another site where taken-for-granted Chinese rituals emerge is the family shrine or temple in the garden. Fa Zhou is seen there performing ancestor worship. In the wake of Mu-lan's disguise, transparent spirits of ancestors hold council as to how to prevent Mulan from "dishonoring" the family. After Mulan's feat of res-cuing the emperor and killing Shan-Yu, the ancestors at the temple (sig-naled by Mushu's "Call out for egg rolls!") burst into rap music and dance, the background for the closing credits. In the same vein as the mul-ticultural violence of handcuffing yellowface with black English, Disney fills the old bottle of Orientalist images with not-so-new teen dreams.

Animating Teen Dreams

Billed as family entertainment, Disney's animations appeal to all age groups. Children are, of course, the main consumers of Disney products. In the case of *Mulan,* months prior to its release in movie theaters in the summer of 1998, an entire array of products — toys, stuffed animals, clothes, backpacks, paper cups, paper napkins, and so forth — flooded the market, culminating in the animation itself. Although the cartoon may be the centerpiece, it is but one of Disney's marketing strategies that capitalize on the image of an Oriental girl stamped on every product. For children to acquire a piece of this Orientalist fantasy, adults must be persuaded to purchase it, a transaction of money and commodity, of desire and symbol, that implicates both children and adults. More-over, it is unlikely that children would frequent movie theaters without parental escort. Even when the videocassette of Disney animation is played, at times to baby-sit children, adults may steal a glance or two at the TV screen.

Beyond practical considerations of commodity consumption, the magic of the Magic Kingdom lies squarely in fantasies of the teenage years, fantasies shared by children and adults alike. Although viewed cultur-ally as a transitional period when much unease and self-doubt are felt, adolescence remains the ideal age, glamorized in the slim, anorexic bod-ies of fashion models and fetishized in the coolness of a Leonardo Di-Caprio on the silver screen. Each generation of moviegoers, of course, hails its own DiCaprio, celluloid teen idols whose grandfather is James

Dean. Freud's "Creative Writers and Day-Dreaming" helps to illuminate the fascination with teens. As a child grows, Freud maintains, "he stops playing, gives up nothing but the link with real objects; instead of *playing*, he now *phantasies* [*sic*]." Freud proceeds to dissect the difference between children's play and adults' fancy:

> A child's play is determined by... the wish to be big and grown up.... On the one hand, he [the adult] knows that he is expected not to go on playing or phantasying any longer, but to act in the real world; on the other hand, some of the wishes which give rise to his phantasies are of a kind which it is essential to conceal. Thus he is ashamed of his phantasies as being childish and as being unpermissible. (438)

Part of the "unpermissible" fantasies of transgression lie in Disney's — for lack of a better term — antifamily undercurrents, despite its self-promotion as family entertainment with family values. Nearly all Disney characters are from impaired or dysfunctional families: Mulan has a crippled father and has to substitute for him in battle; Pocahontas, Little Mermaid, Jasmine, and Belle grow up without mothers; Simba's father is stampeded to death; Snow White and Sleeping Beauty endure cruel stepmothers; Bambi and the gypsy Esmeralda in *The Hunchback of Notre Dame* (1996) are orphans. Such widespread absence of parents can be interpreted as both children's and as adults' desire for autonomy. In either case, family members sitting next to oneself have to be extinguished, at least temporarily, clandestinely in the dark isolation of a theater. It is tempting to decipher this recurring motif of bereavement as highlighting the importance of family via its absence, but Disney's happy ending never involves the formation of new families by protagonists. Characters are formulaically teenagers engaged in premarital romance — no family, no children, no responsibility. Whenever characters unite after great travail, the animation ends and they never become married couples. A marriage would mean not only family obligation but a cessation of the youthful adventures outside of parental supervision just experienced by audiences of all ages.

As a result, Disney's target audience, the children, openly dreams of growing up into teenagers; the adults secretly dream of regressing into teenagers. The former group wishes to empower itself by romanticizing teens, such as Wendy and her brothers taking flight with Peter Pan; the latter wishes to shirk responsibility and a lifetime of disenchantment through a nostalgic look backward, such as Wendy's father reminiscing his winged days at the conclusion of *Peter Pan* (1953). From either direction, adolescence is seen as a time of looking cool, of experiencing adventures away from home, and of finding self-identity. Disney's decision to highlight the trio of teen dreams in *Mulan* is unequivocally exposed when contextualized with the animation's unacknowleged source of inspiration, Kingston, as well as with Kingston's unacknowledged source of inspiration, "The Ballad of Mulan."

The look is paramount to adolescents. Almost all Disney animations feature handsome teenage protagonists, who talk and move like typical American youth. Consider, at the outset, the hair fetish. Belle, in *The Beauty and the Beast* (1991), constantly runs her finger over the lock of hair curled around her forehead. Even the young lion Simba in *The Lion King* (1994) has bangs over his eyes à la Leonardo DiCaprio or Brad Pitt. Although John Smith dubbed by Mel Gibson in *Pocahontas* appears to be more mature, his bangs boast two swirls that could only be stabilized by generous applications of hair gel. The hair fetish in *Mulan* is elevated from a symbol of gorgeous looks to one of gender, the pivotal motif in this story of cross-dressing (figure 29).

When Mulan decides to substitute for her father, she cuts her hair with the masculine symbol of a sword, leaving in place of the conscription scroll her hair comb, a gift from her mother. During her disguise as the recruit Ping, her hair is tied in a bun as with all other Chinese male characters. (By contrast, the "barbarian" invaders of Shan-Yu and his henchmen have long, untied hair.)[2] The only moments when her hair is loosened are when her identity is at risk of being revealed. As she disrobes and unties her hair to bathe in the pond, her colleagues suddenly join her. After the battle, an injured Mulan is in bed, breasts bulging beneath bandages and hair soon to be loosened, at which time her masquerade comes to an abrupt end. In subsequent scenes, Mulan sports loosened hair for she has been uncovered. In order to bait Shan-Yu and save a fainted Shang, Mulan pulls back her hair to reveal her former self. Mulan's alter ego, the girl doll, likewise has long hair waving in the wind. On the snowy grave of Shang's father, against the sword and helmet that serve as the tombstone, Mulan leaves the doll. The proximity of the masculine sword and the feminine long hair foreshadows Mulan's imminent danger in battles against Shan-Yu and against Chinese patriarchy. Also, with this ritual to commemorate the dead, both Shang and Mulan are cut loose from their past, growing into "man-

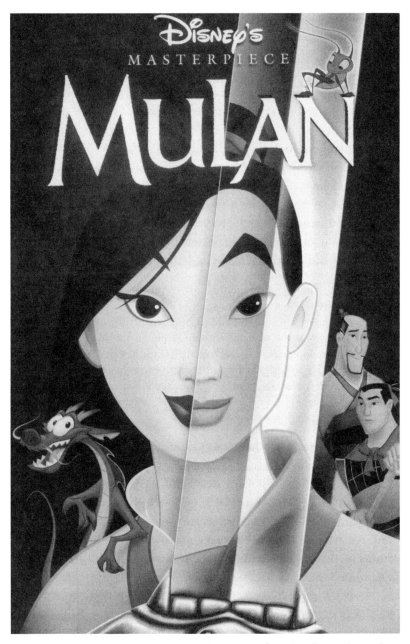

Figure 29. *Mulan* in videocasette. Cross-dressing is reflected in the two hairstyles, partly seen through the transparent sword. This video case design also features Fa Zhou, Shang, Mushu, and Cri-Kee.

hood"—a general and a male soldier. Although it is prominently displayed in a number of scenes, the doll is largely forgotten in the bulk of the animation. Structurally, the doll resembles a Freudian slip, a revealing yet somewhat awkward detail. It materializes out of, literally, thin air, as Shan-Yu's falcon returns from a reconnaissance and drops it into the chieftain's hand. Just as it reappears beside the grave, the doll is destined to be buried in the snowstorm.

Always looking cool, Disney protagonists such as Mulan experience adventures to satisfy a shared human longing, adventures found outside of parental guidance and outside of home. A G-rated film, it turns out, smuggles in, subconsciously, a message about the cessation of family. The dearth of reflection on the part of Disney's family consumers over this and many other blatantly contradictory elements is predicted by Horkheimer and Adorno in *Dialectic of Enlightenment* (1944):

> Real life is becoming indistinguishable from the movies. The sound
> film . . . leaves no room for imagination or reflection on the part of the
> audience, who is unable to respond within the structure of the film, yet
> deviate[s] from its precise detail without losing the thread of the story;
> hence the film forces its victims to equate it directly with reality. . . . [The
> sound films] are so designed that quickness, powers of observation, and
> experience are undeniably needed to apprehend them at all; yet
> sustained thought is out of the question if the spectator is not to miss
> the relentless rush of facts. (126–27)

This is a bleak vision of what Horkheimer and Adorno call "the culture industry" epitomized by movies. One way to escape from the tyranny of filmic images lies in slowing down the "rush," in lengthening each moment by means of a historicist juxtaposition with earlier texts. History or time then derails the breathless presentness of Disney animations. For instance, the contemporary-ness of *Mulan*—its appeal to teen dreams of the 1990s—becomes readily apparent when one contrasts *Mulan* with Kingston's *The Woman Warrior* and with "The Ballad of Mulan." A key moment of *Mulan* occurs when Mulan transforms herself into a male soldier. Animation at its best, this sequence with no dialogue develops visually through fast-paced action of Mulan cutting her hair and stealing away, punctuated by an exciting sound track. This sequence is preceded by a defiant Mulan storming away from the family dinner table and, subsequently, curled up beneath the dragon statue, soaking wet. Upon reaching a decision, Mulan walks barefoot into the family shrine to undergo her conversion. Although set in an exotic locale, each episode closely mirrors the routine behavior of rebellious teenagers — slouching and pouting alone, tiptoeing to sneak off. In addition, the sequence is achieved by means of MTV techniques, such as "quick cuts" and "funky camera angles" (Owen 5), the latter most apparent in the "tracking shot" of nothing but Mulan's bare feet walking into the family temple.

However, this "running-away" sequence radically deviates from the Chinese poem "The Ballad of Mulan" as well as from Kingston. "The Ballad" depicts Mulan's substitution as a family decision rather than a solo performance. The poem opens with a distraught Mulan at the spinning wheel, who responds to the question of the cause of her sadness as follows:

> "Last night I saw the draft list —
> The Khan's mustering a great army;
> The armies' rosters ran many rolls,
> Roll after roll held my father's name!
> And Father has no grown-up son,
> And I've no elder brother!
> So I offered to buy a saddle and horse
> And campaign from now on for Father."
>
> In the eastern market she bought a steed,
> At the western a saddle and cloth;
> In the southern market she bought a bridle,
> At the northern a long whip;
> At sunrise she bade her parents farewell,
> At sunset she camped by the Yellow River;
> She couldn't hear her parents calling her,
> She heard only the Yellow River's flow surge and splash.
> (Liu and Lo 78)

Mulan volunteers "to buy a saddle and horse / And campaign from now on for Father" in answer to an unknown interlocutor. Although one is at liberty to interpret the quotation marks surrounding the first stanza cited above as indications of Mulan's interior monologue, the second stanza intensifies the sense of social interaction through an exchange of ideas. The purchase of a horse and other equipment befitting a recruit is most likely engaged in by the family as a whole, considering how paltry a young unmarried woman's private funds must have been, if she had any at all, in the sixth century A.D. Mulan then bids farewell to her parents and her thoughts return to her parents in "She couldn't hear her parents calling her," which is repeated in the following stanza. The line "At sunrise she bade her parents farewell" is somehow mistranslated by Arthur Waley as "In the morning she stole from her father's and mother's house" (113). The original Chinese reads "*tsao tz'u yeh niang chu*," literally translated as "morning — bid farewell — father — mother — leave." The key word is *tz'u*, "bid farewell," which indicates that Mulan does not furtively run away from home. Unless Waley bases his rendition on an entirely different version of "The Ballad," it is surprising that such a renowned sinologist could have made such an error.

Waley furnishes the only support Disney could possibly marshal to justify its presentation of a Mulan leaving surreptitiously in the wee hours of the morning, which assumes that Disney was aware of the existence of this ballad. Moreover, Mulan Disney reveals her true pedigree by devoting herself, like most of her animated siblings, to a series of carefree adventures, totally blocking out her worried parents. Mulan Disney has, in a manner of speaking, turned her back on the very meaning of the tale of Mulan in China. The Mu Lan legend has long been regarded as one of the many deeds of filial piety. For instance, the illustrated *Hundred Tales of Filial Piety* by Chang Tse-tung of the Ching dynasty features a Mu Lan surnamed Wei instead of Hua. The acts of *hsiao* or filial piety promoted by Chang and others tend to be masochistic sacrifices, such as defrosting a hole on a frozen river with one's bare torso in order to catch a fish for the stepmother, or feeding mosquitoes with one's naked body so that the parents can sleep undisturbed. The former hero eventually becomes a high-ranking government official, the latter a Taoist master. In the Confucian thought, these characters embody the basis of the moral code — filial piety, out of which springs an ordered, highly stratified human society. While retaining the theme of self-sacrifice, Disney has excised the heavy didactic, moralistic tone of the Chinese Mulan.

Even the other American Mulan, Kingston's phantasmic woman warrior in her chapter titled "White Tigers," in *The Woman Warrior*, fails to live up to Disney's amnesiac escapade. The apprentice of martial arts in Kingston is so homesick that she is allowed to look into a magic gourd for her parents. Furthermore, on the eve of the woman warrior setting out on behalf of her father, Kingston deliberately transposes the tale of the Sung dynasty general Yueh Fei onto Fa Mu Lan. (Kingston spells the name differently from Disney and from "The Ballad.") In other words, the tattoo of Mu Lan's back with sacred vows of revenge belongs originally to the legend of Yueh Fei. "[My father] began cutting; to make fine lines and points he used thin blades, for the stems, large blades," narrates Kingston. "My mother caught the blood and wiped the cuts with a cold towel soaked in wine. It hurt terribly — the cuts sharp; the air burning; the alcohol cold, then hot" (*The Woman Warrior* 41). With the meticulous depiction of its gradations, the excruciating pain inflicted upon the woman warrior by her parents signifies the anguish of identity-formation for minorities in the 1970s. Deemed too "gross" for a young audience, Disney proceeds to turn the only inscription in the film into Mulan writing calligraphy on her wrist in hopes of outwitting the matchmaker's standard questions. In chronological order, an anonymous poet in the sixth century A.D. sings of Mulan's filial piety and patriotism; similar traditional morals inform the tale of Yueh Fei; Mulan is collected in didactic stories of filial piety to edify the public throughout various dynasties; a Chinese American novelist grafts the twins of Mu Lan and Yueh Fei as a trope for ethnic and feminist identity; Disney's animation accentuates the clandestine playfulness of gender reversal and adolescent adventures away from home.

The same transformations across time occur in Disney's battle scene. The charge of the barbarians and the ensuing avalanche are stunningly real, a panoramic spectacle of computer-generated virtual reality. The fighting, however, is absent in "The Ballad," inhabiting literally the space between two stanzas:

> After a hundred battles the generals are dead,
> Ten years now, and the brave soldiers are returning!
>
> Returning to audience with the Son of Heaven,
> The Son of Heaven, sitting in his Luminous Hall.
> . . . .
> Then the Khan asked what Mulan desired. (78)

On the other hand, the battles in Kingston unfold in the tradition of martial arts and the *wu-hsia* film genre. Concurrent with Mu Lan's growth as a formidable general, her femininity grows as well in terms of the fetus in her womb inside her enlarged armor.

The woman warrior's clashes with her enemies culminate in the enthroning of the people's emperor in the Forbidden City. An ancient story acquires a modern twist:

> I stood on top of the last hill before Peiping ... the land was peopled — the Han people, the People of One Hundred Surnames, marching with one heart, our tatters flying. The depth and width of joy were exactly known to me: the Chinese population. . . . [The people] inaugurated the peasant who would begin the new order. In his rags he sat on the throne facing south and we, a great red crowd, bowed to him three times. (50)

Kingston has, in this scene, overlapped several images of Tiananmen fresh in the collective memory of her 1970s American readership: Mao Zedong's announcement of the founding of the People's Republic of China in 1949 and the surging Red Guards' chanting of "Long Live Chairman Mao!" during the height of the Cultural Revolution. Moreover, the novelist ingeniously blends such recent events of proletarian mass movements with the dynastic traditions of "the throne facing south."

The teen dreams that Disney perpetuates are part of the youth consumer culture. As a result, *Mulan* simulates some of the cinematic conventions in Hollywood. The archvillain Shan-Yu is disposed of by Mulan via a firecracker that resembles a rocket, hence the amalgamation of Orientalist icons and contemporary filmic clichés in action thrillers. Stabbed in the stomach by the rocket, a phallic symbol, Shan-Yu lifts off into the air, thus recycling the incredible ending of villains being speared and carried away by rockets, such as the demise of John Travolta in John Woo's *Broken Arrow* (1996). Prior to the rocket attack, Mulan frames the position of Shan-Yu with her fingers like a professional photographer, underlining her coolness in the face of monstrosity. Broadly speaking, the party culture of adolescents is made to infect even ancestors' spirits at the conclusion of *Mulan*; phantoms in classical Chinese costume break out into dance in consonance with rap music. Likewise, the longing for romance dictates that Shang seek out Mulan, at the urging of the emperor.

Teen dreams revolve around, as Freud puts it, "growing up" or fashioning self-identity. For the majority of white, Gen-X audience to see themselves in Mulan's self-discovering saga and identify with her, they must find race and, for half of the audience, gender transparent. Chineseness in *Mulan* is presented as exotic dresses to be tried on by spectators, as role-playing, neither of which poses soul-searching, gut-wrenching deconstruction of one's subjectivity. A perfect analogy is Americans' love affair with Barbie dolls. The series of Barbie collectibles includes Barbie the Chinese Empress, modeled after the Ching dynasty's Empress Dowager, in Manchurian dress, cap, accessories, and a darker skin tone. This Chinese Empress's sisters include Barbie the French Lady and a host of other racialized dolls. The fascination with Barbie stems from the ease of transmutations of the self, an entity of consciousness projected by the doll owner onto the doll's naked body. There appear to be as many Barbies as there are her apparels, yet Barbie remains fundamentally unchanged in her smile and her fashion-model figure. As a consequence, the doll owner is able to assume multiple roles in imagination, facilely and superficially, just as Barbie is made to change into her sundry outfits. For that matter, Disney's 1990s characters, despite their divergent racial backgrounds, exhibit an amazing degree of similarity physically and temperamentally. The French Belle of 1991 resembles the Arab Jasmine of 1992, who resembles the Native American Pocahontas of 1995, who resembles the gypsy Esmeralda of 1996, who resembles the Greek Meg of 1997, who resembles the Chinese Mulan of 1998. Disney's dominant genes dictate the look and the behavior of his brood of idealized adolescents, whereas race and culture become, ironically, recessive genes. To illustrate Disney's subsuming of race and culture into adolescent desires, one turns to the scene of fireworks and dragon dance at what appears to be the Hall of Supreme Harmony (*Taihedian*) at the heart of Beijing's Forbidden City in — not *Mulan* but *Aladdin*. This fleeting glimpse — along with those of the Taj Mahal, the Parthenon in the Acropolis, the Jefferson Memorial, and other famous sites — provides the backdrop for the teen romance unfolding between Aladdin and Jasmine on the magic carpet traveling through time and space.

Indeed, Disney has exploited Orientalist images as racial markers. What follows is an investigation of Disney's strategies of racial dichotomy between us and them, between the Hans and the Huns. American moviegoers instinctively take the side of the "good guys," the Hans defending themselves, a natural human reaction to any alleged struggle of the virtuous against the evil. Race and gender differences of the characters from the audience are elided in an abstract identification with the good. This is not to deny the spellbinding "power of the dark side," as James Earl Jones intones in his black cape and helmet in *Star Wars*. Before one plunges into race, however, it is important to reiterate Mulan's search for a new gender, which constitutes nothing less than a fun-filled game for both boys and girls. To act like a man, Mulan has to learn to walk, talk, spit, and fight. The awkwardness of this process is exemplified in her hesitation and stammer before naming herself "Ping," popularized as masculine through *Turandot* but sounding equally feminine to Chinese ears. Masculinity becomes a role that Mulan assumes, in the same way that Caucasian youngsters would identify with a Chinese-looking yet American-acting Mulan.

To empathize with the Hans, the dominant Chinese race, the audience must be made to reject the other—the Hun invaders. The polarization of race manifests itself in the Huns' gray skin tone and in the Hans' fairer skin tone. Disney accomplishes this further by rendering Shan-Yu and his followers as animalistic, predatory barbarians. With fingers like a hawk's talons, the steep forehead of a gorilla, eyes and eyebrows squashed together, and two pointed snake fangs, Shan-Yu is, arguably, simian. He hangs upside down like an ape; he scales the Great Wall and climbs trees; he sniffs at the doll that his falcon brings back from its scouting. With his superhuman strength, he bursts out of snow that annihilates his entire army except for his closest comrades. His henchmen subsequently penetrate the palace, hidden inside the dancing dragon, a Chinese Trojan horse in mockery of the emperor's symbol.

Of course, Disney did not initiate the portrayal of the Huns as "barbarians"; the Han Chinese have historically done that. The genre of "frontier poetry" in Tang poetry is replete with Chinese soldiers stationed near the northern border defending against the aliens on the other side of the Great Wall. Even contemporary Chinese continue to refer to China as the fusion of five "tsu" or peoples: Hans, Manchurians, Mongolians, Muslims, and Tibetans. Naming themselves after the two most glorious dynasties in history—Han (206 B.C.–A.D. 220) and Tang (A.D. 618–907)—Chinese hegemony is closely tied to the Hans. Although "The Ballad" does not allude to any specific dynasty in Chinese history, Mulan does say that she only wishes to be given a "fleet-footed camel" to take her back to her parents rather than be awarded the post of "shan-shu-lan," a post closely associated with the Han dynasty. "Shan-shu" was created during the Chin dynasty and continued in Han.

Although the Chinese have historically segregated the Hans and the Huns, Westerners have bought into this easy distinction with their usual fervor over things Oriental. Puccini's *Turandot* opens with the conflict between Turandot the heartless princess of Peking and her foreign suitors. The Prince of Persia is about to be executed for failing to answer Turandot's three riddles. Calif, yet another enraptured by Turandot's icy beauty, has a name derived from the title of the secular and religious ruler of a Muslim state, hence a royal figure from a foreign land. Turandot in fact turns vengeful and sadistic because of her female ancestor Princess Lou-Ling, who was ravished by "the King of the Tartars." Evidently, "Persia," "Muslim," and "Tartars" are all synonyms of the Huns to Puccini. In splitting the Hans and the Huns, neither the Chinese nor the Westerner heeds the textual evidence within "The Ballad" suggesting that Mulan may be bicultural, if not biracial.

In "The Ballad," Mulan states that "The Khan's mustering a great army," referring to the Han Son of Heaven ("*Tien-tse*") rather than the Khan of the northern nomadic tribes. Similarly, Mulan switches between "The Son of Heaven, sitting in his Luminous Hall" and "the Khan asked what Mulan desired." The fluidity of addresses points to a hybridized subjectivity of Mulan's, of her anonymous author's, or of both. The imported term *Khan,* adopted side by side with the Chinese term *Son of Heaven,* suggests the northern tribal origin or culture of the character in the ballad and/or of the person composing it. Indeed, a footnote in Liu and Lo's *Sunflower Splendor* (1975) says that Mulan came from "northern, i.e., non-Chinese, stock and lived during the Six Dynasties period (A.D. 220–588)" (77 n. 1). The Chinese have conveniently cleansed Mulan of her adulterated cultural and perhaps racial background, an enterprise of essentialization intensified in Kingston and in Disney for their own ends.

Part IV
Masquerading of Ethnicity

CHAPTER EIGHT

Kazuo Ishiguro's Persistent Dream for Postethnicity

Performance in Whiteface

"Why, Mr. Stevens, why, why, why do you always have to *pretend*?"
— Kazuo Ishiguro, *The Remains of the Day* 154

Although some critics may find it devilishly inappropriate, even unprofessional, to confuse fictitious characters and the fiction writer, surely no one would dispute the simple fact that being figments of the imagination, characters could be viewed as a novelist's projections of his or her unique conditions of existence, ethnicity being one of them. Therefore, just as a desperate Miss Kenton poses the question above to Stevens, who has managed to ignore her love for years, I ask Kazuo Ishiguro the same question concerning his own performance, a career that barely touches on his Anglo-Japanese ethnicity. This is to assume, in an essentialist manner, that there is such a thing — a particular kind of ethnicity — to be represented. But to assume otherwise is a luxury enjoyed by "the haves," who have moved beyond the basic struggles for civil rights, whose ethnicity is no longer an impediment to success, whose ethnicity, in an ironic twist, is the key to success in a West fond of tokenized minorities. Moreover, though there appears to be only one Anglo-Japanese character in Ishiguro's corpus of four novels, he may very well be dealing with his own ethnicity all along. That he never locates the central consciousness of his novels in Anglo-Japanese but vacillates between Japanese and English characters testifies to the intangible subject position of minorities in the West, a position so laden with minority dis-ease that one rushes to join seemingly wholesome, well-integrated, and immutable identities. As such, the likes of the butler Stevens in *The Remains of the Day* (1989) and of the pianist Ryder in *The Unconsoled* (1995) suggest not only *reaction* against readers' ethnic stereotypes generated by Ishiguro's two earlier "Japanese" novels, but *reactionary* cooptation into a dreamworld of postethnicity. The minority complex over how one's differences are being perceived and received by others is projected by Ishiguro onto the majority, specifically Stevens and Ryder, whose professions consist of public performances that put private selves under erasure. Yet the suppression of ethnicity, as any suppression goes, is attended by tremendous tension, which in turn is cloaked by the increasing stylization of Ishiguro's four books. Stylization seeks to generalize and ritualize, thereby minimizing individual variations. The behavior of a butler or of a renowned musician then proceeds in accordance with idealized social codes. While Ishiguro's characters always suffer from concealment of secret lives, his English protagonists have grown obsessed with mannerisms and public personae. His characters' denial of emotions parallels a minority writer's innermost neurosis, a deep-seated anxiety over identity. In terms of language, the perfect, precise British English in which every character speaks, Japanese included, and with which every scene is laid out totalizes the novel, so much so that characters and scenes become no more than mouthpieces and backdrops for Ishiguro's overarching concern for the human condition. Any commentary with so sweeping a scope betrays a desire to exceed one's limitations, such as ethnicity. It is worth noting that all of his books explore the failure of such a desire.

Subversive Whiteface Reacting against Orientalism

Kazuo Ishiguro's career destabilizes one of the most pressing issues of our time—ethnicity—underscoring at once its gravity and its fleetingness. Intrinsic merits of his novels aside, minority concerns in England and the industrialized First World in the 1980s catapult into prominence the Ishiguro of the two "Japanese" novels—*A Pale View of Hills* (1982) and *An Artist of the Floating World* (1986). Without the apparently ethnic themes and characters, without Ishiguro's own Japanese name and face on the book covers, the novelist speculates in an interview that he would have had a much tougher time breaking through.[1] However, Ishiguro's ethnicity is attributed to him on the essentialist premises of the Japanese culture he inherits from his family and the Japanese fictional universe he in turn creates. His third novel, *The Remains of the Day,* by contrast, appears almost Conradian in its being more English than the English. As if taunting his readers' assumption of race and ethnicity, Ishiguro conjures up an idealized England of the past decades through the eyes of a British butler, rather than those of Etsuko, the Japanese immigrant in the British Isles in *Pale,* or of Masuji Ono, the Japanese painter in Japan in *Artist.* Indeed, *Remains* proceeds almost entirely devoid of any Asian reference, with the exception of the porcelain Chinaman adorning the staircase at Darlington Hall. *The Unconsoled* outdoes the de-ethnicized *Remains* by anchoring itself in the dreams and nightmares, not even in the daytime interior monologue, of an Englishman. An ethnic writer's persistent desire for *post*ethnicity is eventually realized in *The Unconsoled,* cast, ironically, as a dream, one that emanates minority anxiety because it pretends to be its opposite—the majority. The very form of *The Unconsoled* suggests that postethnicity is a wish fulfillment and the deracinated dreamscape a reaction against Orientalist readings of his "Japanese" novels. But could it not be possible that Ishiguro's ethnicity is as much an ideological construct of our own making as postethnicity is of Ishiguro's? Does it not stand to reason that the Japaneseness perceived in the novelist in fact resembles the Englishness in Stevens and in Ryder?

Such mutual dreaming of fictitious characters, of fiction writers, and of fiction readers brings to mind the Chinese philosopher Chuang-tzu (fifth to fourth century b.c.), who "dreamt that he was a butterfly.... Suddenly he awakened, and there he was, veritably Chuang Chou [Chou was his personal name] himself. Now he does not know whether the butterfly is a dream of Chuang Chou or whether Chuang Chou is a dream of the butterfly" (Liu 41). Chuang-tzu problematizes the self by shifting subjectivity from the human to an insect, hence to the entire world. But the fact that we attribute such erasure of self to Chuang-tzu rather than to a butterfly highlights Chuang-tzu's personal philosophy. The abandonment of the self can only derive from a self strong enough to be abandoned. Similarly, Ishiguro's Stevens and Ryder appear to be divorced from the author's background, but they only materialize, like sculptures on a totem pole, on the shoulders of Etsuko and of Ono. Ishiguro's persistent dream for universalist parables beyond identity politics arises from his firm grounding in the literary scene via his ethnic "stage." Postethnicity seems to be an excess indulged in only by those who have already made it, partly by virtue of their ethnicity.

To be fair to Ishiguro, the critical side of him in various published interviews and colloquiums has vehemently resisted being categorized as an ethnic writer. He has cautioned against any comparison with contemporaries such as Salman Rushdie and Timothy Mo, two among many English writers of non-English descent.[2] He has repeatedly pointed out the absurdity and racism of being associated with Japanese writers such as Mishima and Tanizaki. Yasujiro Ozu is perhaps the only Japanese master to whom he regularly pays tribute. But he has credited not just Ozu's postwar films of *shomin-geki* (domestic drama) but Chekhov's plays for his daring experimentation in the sluggish movement or utter plotlessness of his stories.[3] Most significantly, he has emphasized his creative drive of shuttling between the specific and the metaphorical, between realism and allegory, between matter-of-fact details and the universal. In other words, Ishiguro has insisted throughout his career on being regarded as postethnic *as well.* Although he never disavows the ethnic-specific nature of some of his works, he tirelessly brings up their universal aspect. It is intriguing to note that such persistence has culminated thus far in the surrealist *The Unconsoled,* whose dreamscape evokes the modernist angst of Kafka, the surrealist paintings of Salvador Dalí, the mazelike lithographs of M. C. Escher, and a host of other, for lack of a better term, "universalist aestheticians." To be sure, scholars have explored, among other subjects, Kafka's Jewish background and Dalí's roots in the devastation of the Great War. The fact remains, however, that these artists had opted for an artistic expression that was deliberately abstract and universal, supposedly above and beyond the mundane world they critiqued. The three melted timepieces in the bleak wasteland of Dalí's 1931 *The Persistence of Memory,* for instance, try to deny memory but eerily revalidate it. Time is suspended, distance warped, intentions thwarted, all of which echo perfectly the mood of *The Unconsoled.* But by merely distorting and not annihilating time, distance, and intentions, Dalí and Ishiguro in effect call attention to these mutations. Despite one's attempt to undo memory, it returns with greater force. The corpses of timepieces no longer tell the time; they haunt it. Each of Ishiguro's protagonists is likewise locked in the prison house of memory, the web of which constitutes and arrests the self. All his male

characters tried or continue to try to rise above mediocrity, or the con-
fines of the self, for the noble cause of ameliorating the human condition. Ono, Lord Darlington and his shadow, Stevens, and Ryder were
once or still are trapped by delusions of grandeur, forced in the end to
confront the tragic consequences of their own actions. Their failure has
a certain tragic dignity to it, reflecting Ishiguro's own dream for transcending ethnicity.

But before pronouncing dead the postethnic text of *The Unconsoled,*
we need to reassess exactly how his first two novels come to be charac-
terized as "Japanese" and why *Remains* comes off as a huge success with
its equally postethnic theme. Despite the universalist claims in his interviews, Ishiguro's first two books are thoroughly stamped with ethnic
markers. Both Etsuko and Ono are coping with their personal trans-
gressions deeply intertwined with Japan's recent past. Etsuko neglected
and even abused her own daughter in postwar Nagasaki, resulting in
the daughter's alienation and eventual suicide in England.[4] Ono dedicated his artistic talents to Japanese military expansionism, and was thus
personally responsible for the disaster of World War II. Ishiguro, nevertheless, did not compose these stories solely from firsthand experiences
of Japan. He left Nagasaki with his family for England in 1960 when he
was five or six years old. Images of homeland retained by a young child
are bound to be vague and limited, yet Ishiguro finds a way to capitalize on what is presumably a weakness in fiction writing. By having his
protagonists explore their shaky recall of the past, Ishiguro ingeniously
justifies the fuzziness of Japan in his own creative mind. Consequently,
the hills near Nagasaki as well as the past associated with it, remembered
by a guilt-ridden mother, become a "pale view" with indistinct outlines.
The retired painter Ono, far more admirable than Etsuko in acknowl-
edging his mistakes, rambles on, apparently indiscriminately, about a
world in constant flux. Despite the appearance of sharp rifts in his own
career and in Japan's history, the novel is an amazingly coherent jum-
ble of images and sounds, one interweaving with the other to formulate
a complete life story, a mosaic of sorts of muted tones and smudged
contours. Ono's "flow" through an ever-changing world comes through
in the thematic repetitions of betrayals. The young artistic Ono rebels
against his businessman father by joining an art company that mass-
produces Orientalist kitsch for foreign consumption. But such a revolt
continues the family tradition of mercantilism. Ono subsequently deserts

art as a business for Mori-san's art for art's sake, indulging himself in the ephemeral "Pleasure District." Awakened by patriotism and social concerns, Ono abandons his *sensei*'s principles and unwittingly joins the fascist militarists. In the process, he betrays to the authorities his own less royalist disciple, Kuroda, who languishes in prison during the war. It is significant that the partings with both Mori-san and Kuroda are set in the same pavilion, accentuating the pattern of repetition in his life. In fact, in his old age, Ono increasingly speaks and thinks like Mori-san, whom he discredited in his youth. The antagonism Kuroda's student, Enchi, exhibits toward Ono parallels Ono's earlier resentment against Mori-san.

It is in such duplications of events within a vaguely ethnic context that one must see the kindling of the postethnic impulse, for repetitions signal a general condition rather than unique characteristics. Indeed, Ishiguro, for autobiographical reasons, could not afford to be otherwise. Part of him is English, even international, and decidedly un-Japanese. He seeks to extricate himself from identity politics by means of not only the recurring events in Ono's life but by having characters such as Ono resurrected as a British lord, a butler, and a pianist, not to mention his previous reincarnation as the father-in-law, the equally nationalist Ogata-san, in *Pale*. What Ono experiences resembles what many characters undergo, regardless of racial difference. In addition to the string of aging, self-deluded males, young boys likewise take after one another. The spoiled, whiny Japanese boy Akira of *Pale* finds his own mirror image in the grandson Ichiro of *Artist,* subsequently transformed into the overweight, sulky Boris of *The Unconsoled.* Characters are carryovers from one book to the next because the fundamental human emotions explored through them are identical, namely, an inconsolable guilt and emptiness. Despite Etsuko's whitewashing of her past, despite Ono's courage and goodwill toward the new Japan, despite Stevens's bracing for the remainder of his days, despite Ryder's keeping up of appearances, their lives are revealed to be irrevocably devoid of human warmth. To some extent, this preoccupation with the shared human condition accounts for some reviewers' complaint about the lack of individuality in Ishiguro's characters, who are likened, rather mean-spiritedly by Louis Menand, to "papier-mâché animations" (3) operating according to some technical manual on gradations of human emotions.

This thematic refrain culminates and intensifies in Ishiguro's most recent novel, a refrain that so irritates certain reviewers that they parody the title as "uncontrolled," "unrelenting." Jeff Giles describes it as "dull, repetitious, long-winded, long-winded, repetitious, dull.... It's as if he got sick of reading about how compact his prose is — how he's the poet laureate of the unspoken and the unexpressed — and suddenly retaliated with his dense snowstorm of words" (92F). Will Blythe agrees that "fatigue sets in because *The Unconsoled* is curiously one-dimensional.... The novel successfully embodies the dream logic of the unconscious, but that seems to be all it does" (65). This damning assessment is echoed by Ned Rorem: "The situation, a bad dream from which Ryder will never awake, is Kafka in reverse.... But at least Kafka is concise and visionary, whereas Ishiguro is directionless and undifferentiated" (157). Other reviewers see this, nevertheless, as an accomplishment. Tom Wilhelmus maintains that "Ishiguro has created a monument to boredom, accident, indifference, obtuseness, pretension, and misunderstanding — a great negative adventure that is at once darkly humorous and a striking moral commentary.... The effect is Kafkaesque, a swirling mixture of inexplicable guilt and dislocation in time" (322). Francis Wyndham likewise reports that the book is "not easy to read, but, surprisingly, its overall effect does contain an element of consolation. The muddle, panic, embarrassment, and dread that surface in our secret dreams do also, needless to say, feature in our daytime lives, and it is some comfort to be reminded by Ishiguro that they are universal" (94).

If one disregards the differences of opinion in these reviews and focuses instead on the evolution of Ishiguro's postethnic concerns, then the novelist has largely succeeded. To contextualize *The Unconsoled*, reviewers draw from Kafka, Lewis Carroll, Luis Buñuel, and no longer Mishima, Tanizaki, Ozu. It is perhaps not surprising that *Remains* and *The Unconsoled*, their shared postethnic world notwithstanding, should elicit such different responses, with reviewers overwhelmingly in favor of the former. *Remains* won the Booker Prize in 1989 and was turned into a Merchant-Ivory film starring Anthony Hopkins and Emma Thompson. Evidently, the realistic *Remains* proves to be a far less disorienting read than its surrealistic successor. The irony is that whereas the England of *Remains* may appear to exist comfortably in time, the book's appeal stems from the public's nostalgia for a bygone era imagined to have existed. On the other hand, though the restless nightmares of *The Unconsoled* seem to occur outside time, they in effect reflect much of the reader's life experiences — a colossal exercise in futility, anticipation followed, almost without fail, by disenchantment. Ultimately, it may be the lack of anchoring or contextualizing in *The Unconsoled* — which is of course Ishiguro's whole point — that dooms the novel. And yet, one can argue that it is precisely because Ishiguro moors his book too securely in life that the reader refuses to endorse the vision of "Horror! Horror!" The circular, continuously frustrated motion of Ryder's itinerary, or the lack thereof, reminds the reader, rather disturbingly, of M. C. Escher's 1951 *House of Stairs,* where interconnected flights of stairs lead into one another, on which crawl and roll centipedes, Sisyphuses lobotomized and robbed of even the consolation of existentialism. Ishiguro's expression is understandably even more difficult for the public to accept than that of Escher's lithograph or, for that matter, Kafka's "Metamorphosis." Whereas his predecessors cast their commentaries in explicitly allegorical terms, those of centipedes or a beetle, Ishiguro never deviates from the human world and never provides any sense of insulation. Ishiguro gives, in the words of Carlton Lake in describing Dalí's "paranoiac-critical method," "the most incongruous or unbelievable material such detail and precision that it acquired, in the process, a life of its own and became almost plausible" (68–69). What dooms the reception of his novel may well be that the "detail and precision" are such that the novel becomes too plausibly the reader's own life.

Reactionary Whiteface Subsuming Differences

Yet neither *Remains* nor *The Unconsoled* is truly postethnic. The Englishness of Stevens and Ryder is, in theory if not in practice, just as ethnic as the Japaneseness of Etsuko and Ono. That one could only claim this on the theoretical plane bears witness to the growing realization, best embodied in George Lipsitz's essay "The Possessive Investment in Whiteness," that whiteness has long remained invisible in, and thus beyond, racial discourse. This invisibility derives from whites' majority status and their control of discourse and material resources. The ethnic group in power is usually less inclined to examine the correlation between its race and its power. Therefore, Ishiguro's shift to English characters and postethnicity may suggest problematics much more troubling than a minority's reaction against identity politics by pigeonholing him as nothing but an Anglo-Japanese. Ethnic writers can conceivably imagine ways to become more, not less, ethnic. Why does ethnicity have to make way for postethnicity, an illegitimate heir that is probably one's own, yet alarmingly white? Why should the ethnic community accept one writer's flirtations with postethnicity, perhaps a code word for "whiteness"?

One hastens to add that it is undoubtedly subversive for a minority to perform in whiteface. Given the long history of blackface minstrelsy in North America and its permutations in Europe, it is heartening to see an Anglo-Japanese assume whiteface. More specifically, given the Fu Manchus, the Charlie Chans, the Madame Butterflies, the Dragon Ladies, and other stereotypical Asian characters impersonated by whites, Ishiguro has rendered an invaluable service in expanding the repertoire of imagination for minorities of Asian descent. This potentially revolutionary act, however, is compromised by the fact that the postethnic bent is so removed from the utopianism and activism of previous decades that it has acquired a color-blind, postmodernist flatness that is tantamount to blindness itself. If one were to take Ryder's Englishness as the signifier of postethnicity, or in Ishiguro's own phrase, of universal parable, the novelist is then caught in a double bind: his reaction against Orientalism has turned reactionary by subsuming racial differences. To defy Orientalist characteristics imposed on him, Ishiguro passes as white. Fundamentally a performance on stage or in real life, such passing can be undertaken by all sides of a multiracial society. But the multidirectional passing does not betoken an egalitarian society; rather, it reflects how slanted the socioeconomic relationship is. When Al Jolson, Eddie Cantor, Mickey Rooney, and others — many of whom are Jewish or Irish — perform in blackface, they do so to entertain the white audience, often at the expense of African American images.[5] When Charles W. Chesnutt writes about blacks passing for whites, blacks conceal their race to obtain better opportunities in a white-dominated society. Passing, for minorities, has historically meant a precarious passage into a semblance of power.

To further explore the temptation of passing for minorities, I draw from Jennifer DeVere Brody in "Hyphen-Nations":

[T]he hyphen *performs* — it is never neutral or natural. Indeed, by performing the mid-point between often conflicting categories, hyphens occupy "impossible" positions. . . . Hyphens are problematic because they cannot stand alone: in fact, they do not "stand" at all; rather, they mark a de-centered if central position that perpetually presents readers with a neither/nor proposition. Hyphens locate intermediate, often invisible, and always shifting spaces between supposedly oppositional binary structures. (149)

Despite Brody's somewhat negative description of hyphenated identity, one lacking in subjectivity, her argument unveils the seemingly insignificant yet richly ambiguous hyphen. The destabilizing of race and ethnicity can indeed germinate from the sliver of space between races, a void belonging to neither, a moment pregnant with infinite possibilities. If attributes supposedly innate to one race can be faked by hyphenated, hybridized individuals, then the intrinsicness of those attributes is subject to question. Racial passing thus highlights how an exterior display rather than some immutable "essence" lies at the heart of the construct of race. In the same deconstructive spirit, Judith Butler's *Gender Trouble* (1990) views gender as a series of public acts. Yet unlike homosexuality, which can be kept closeted or be acknowledged, ethnicity, except in the case of mixed-blood, can never mask itself.

Fiction, of course, is something else. Ishiguro has so far masqueraded as Japanese (Ono), Anglo-Japanese (Etsuko), English (Stevens and Ryder), and vaguely Central European (the townspeople in *The Unconsoled*) characters in Japan, England, and an unidentified part of the Continent. The novelist inhabiting that hyphen has emerged in many roles, but rarely as an Asian minority living in the West, or, to put it in unabashedly essentialist terms, in a subject position similar to his own. The closest Ishiguro gets to his own life experiences seems to be Etsuko, a schizophrenic Anglo-Japanese widow in England. Yet even there, Etsuko's narrative hardly ever touches on her experiences in England. The identity of a minority writer receives, in other words, only one oblique treatment through the split personality of Etsuko, as if a talented novelist, confronted with a task most akin to self-representation, resorts to pop psychology, or the banality of a minority's divided self. Even more tellingly, Ishiguro's criticism of *Pale* concentrates on the technical crudeness of his first novel rather than the shallowness of the immigrant protagonist. Describing the moment toward the end of *Pale* whereby Etsuko and Sachiko come to overlap, Ishiguro finds it to be "a shock" and "baffling" (Mason 338) because that finale is ill-prepared by the novel's flashbacks. Ishiguro attributes his discontent with the novel to flashbacks so clear-cut that they are devoid of the "murkiness of someone trying to wade through their [sic] memories, trying to manipulate memories" (337–38). The fusion of the two protagonists appears too artificial and contrived due to, in Ishiguro's own words, his lack of "technical sophistication" (338). It is intriguing that with Ishiguro's acumen, he fails to discern the fundamental flaw of *Pale,* namely, a protagonist poorly delineated in her present surrounding because this would entail building part of the narrative on the slippery pinhead of a hyphen — Ishiguro's own. Ishiguro's career indicates that pins are better used to puncture other bubbles of existence, other constructs of identity.

If Ishiguro's self-diagnosis of unrefined craftsmanship were accurate, he has been remarkable in avoiding similar pitfalls in subsequent novels thriving on the nebulous "texture of memory" (337). His later virtuosity is increasingly accompanied by a distancing from the minority's *specific* positionality, schizophrenic or otherwise, replaced now by everyman's *shared* dilemma between social role and private self. The two English protagonists live a life based on highly stylized public roles, utterly detached from their own feelings and their loved ones. This is not to suggest that public performances do not take place in the "Japanese" novels. But by contrast, both Etsuko and the retired Ono are less public figures than the English protagonists. Etsuko's subconscious confession of her guilt to the daughter Niki and Ono's brave admission of his militarist past during the *miai* (a family meeting in a marriage negotiation) for the second daughter are spontaneous acts to bring the family closer together. If these acts were performance, Etsuko and Ono do them in order to go on living — by reaching out to their family and family-to-be. Stevens and Ryder, on the other hand, come to engage in performances for the sole reason that their lives are but a series of public functions; they perform in order not to live, not to experience the passion and the pain of any human relationship. The growing sense of atomization and alienation in Ishiguro's whitefaces reflects, in a roundabout way, a minority's schizophrenic unease, despite or because of his disguise in fiction. To rephrase Jean-Paul Sartre in *Anti-Semite and Jew* (1948), a minority is someone whom others call a minority. Masquerading as a member of the majority demonstrates at once one's competence and one's deficiency, which calls for the masquerading in the first place. Ishiguro's dream of postethnicity turns out to be a veiling and an intensification of his minority complex.

This minority anxiety festers into the inconsolable hollowness beneath Stevens's and Ryder's public personae. Indeed, they wear the mask so religiously that it grows into their flesh; their total abandonment to social roles arises out of the fear that once the mask is removed, a hole, not a face, will gaze back. Hence Stevens's fixation on exteriority or appearance. As he contemplates a trip to the West Country to visit Miss Kenton, the first thing that comes to mind is, of course, "cost," followed by "costume" (10), or "suitable traveling clothes — that is to say, clothes in which I might be seen driving the car" (11). Paramount in his consideration is propriety, which, for a "gentleman's gentleman," must strike a delicate balance between being seen and staying unseen. Required to dress and behave properly in order to provide services, a butler must, nonetheless, render his presence unnoticeable and unobtrusive. He would look like, but would remain readily distinguishable from, a gentleman. The resemblance to his masters dictates that he must somehow announce himself as a fake. The best way to achieve this is to ape a gentleman while underscoring the inadequacies of such an imitation, an undermining of facade that is bound to be parodic and comical. As a result, Stevens worries about expense and clothes in terms of his material conditions; socially, he is forever concerned with public perception; linguistically, his formal English — phrases like "that is to say" — proclaims its own contrivedness.

Yet in this excursion in search of Miss Kenton, Stevens, for the first time in his life, travels alone, not in the company of a "genuine" gentleman. In the absence of the authentic, the simulacrum not only considers wearing the suit passed on to him by his former employer, Lord Darlington, and motors with the Ford lent to him by his present employer, Mr. Farraday, but momentarily assumes an identity close to that of Lord Darlington. Despite the best attempt at masquerade, everything goes awry. Lord Darlington's dress is too formal and old-fashioned. Stevens is stranded twice because he allows the Ford to go without water and then gasoline. In the second stop at a rural small town, he subconsciously poses as an influential figure once active in "foreign policy" (who has known Churchill, among other celebrities). But his disguise is quickly exposed by Dr. Carlisle, a onetime socialist and a self-exile.

To convince himself that there is more than exteriority, Stevens engages in sophomoric speculations as to the inner quality of a great butler — dignity. Such sporadic intaking of the opium of the mind is submitted, ironically, in the same analogy of a gentleman's suit.

> And let me now posit this: "dignity" has to do crucially with a butler's ability not to abandon the professional being he inhabits. . . . The great butlers are great by virtue of their ability to inhabit their professional role and inhabit it to the utmost; . . . They wear their professionalism as a decent gentleman will wear his suit: . . . he will discard it when, and only when, he wills to do so, and this will invariably be when he is entirely alone. (42–43)

That Stevens must reiterate key words illustrates how hard he is trying to convince himself of the validity of his belief, one that has become dated and irrelevant with the decline of the British Empire, with the sale of Darlington Hall to an American businessman, and with Stevens's own aging. Moreover, even that alleged rupture in a butler's invincible rampart proves to be beyond reach. Miss Kenton has twice tried to approach Stevens when he is alone in his pantry, bringing fresh cuttings and prying into his reading of romantic novels; twice, she is roundly rejected. The mask has imperceptibly grown into his face.

In Stevens's definition of greatness in butlers, the repetitious and circular diction points to a narrow mind. Stevens is imitating the rhetoric of high society such as Lord Darlington's. Indeed, Stevens's "dignity" is derivative of the Lord's "honor," the motto by which the self-appointed diplomat conducts himself. It is no surprise that Stevens would flounder, when the real thing, Lord Darlington, despite his best intentions of honor and fairness, is amateurish, meddling in foreign affairs, being manipulated by Nazi Germany, as Mr. Lewis, the United States senator, declares.[6] In part a social satire, The Remains of the Day derides the hierarchical pyramid based on a descending order of authenticity and greatness. Even the paragon of honor turns out to be a Nazi sympathizer and a pawn of Adolf Hitler.

Just as Stevens is by nature a parodic figure, a clone or duplicate of idealized images, the acclaimed pianist Ryder in The Unconsoled proves himself to be as paltry as the servant. Unlike Stevens, who spends his entire career at Darlington Hall, Ryder, true to his name, tours from one metropolis to the next. Like Lord Darlington, Ryder attempts far more than his capabilities allow — he resolves local disputes tangentially related to music. Most important, Ryder, like Stevens, is so engrossed in performance that he fails to develop any intimate personal relationships. The purported grace of a world-class performer, the equivalent of Stevens's dignity, has permeated Ryder's life to the extent that he could no longer cease to perform, that is, to begin to function according to the dictates of his heart. This cancerous hollowness infects every relationship in *The Unconsoled*: that of Ryder, Sophie, and their child Boris; that of the grandfather Gustav the hotel porter, the daughter Sophie, and the grandson Boris; that of the hotel manager Hoffman, his wife, and their son Stefan; that of the alcoholic conductor Brodsky and his ex-wife Miss Collins. In each of these relationships, couples as well as father and daughter have not spoken to each other for years.

Even the professional facade seems a hoax. When Ryder does perform, he invariably flops. Called upon to identify himself to two provincial women boasting of having met Mr. Ryder, he struggles to pronounce his name until his "face had become bright red and squashed into pig-like features" (240). About to address a large audience, Ryder discovers that his "dressing gown was hanging open, displaying the entire naked front of my body" (143). Standing on a chair to attract attention at another occasion, he is distracted from his speech by Miss Collins. Taking leave of a gallery reception, he mistakes a broom cupboard for the exit, with household mops tumbling down and falling "with a clatter onto the marble floor " (278). Rehearsing his much-awaited pieces, Ryder tries in vain to repair the latch of the practice room, finally hanging up a rag for privacy. His rehearsal at the annex turns out to supply the requiem for the funeral of Brodsky's dog, an event taking place outside the annex unbeknownst to him. By the time he goes on stage, the auditorium has long been cleared and chairs put away. When his authoritative comment on music is solicited, Ryder gives an absolutely ludicrous response, which he judges to be sagacious and well received. *The Unconsoled* is written in such a parodic mode: an elevator ride that allows Gustav to talk nonstop for five pages to a sleepy Ryder;[7] Hoffman's secret hand gesture to Ryder; the townspeople's proposal of a bronze statue in memory of Brodsky's scraggly dog; the amputation of Brodsky's prosthetic leg and his use of an ironing board as a crutch onstage. With these and other episodes squarely in the absurdist and surrealist vein, Kazuo Ishiguro has indeed journeyed far from the intimation of minority subjectivity in his first novel, but the landscape has grown unrecognizable, depressingly dark. One can only wish him well.[8]

Epilogue

I fully understand the contentiousness of my thesis — the deathly embrace of Orientalism and Asian American identity — and that it is likely to elicit strong reactions. But arguing in moderation is simply out of the question if one is to engage in a deconstructing of ethnic identity, as I point out in the Introduction. It is hoped that passion will not be mistaken for vitriol.

A possible criticism of this book is that I focus exclusively on what I term the "discursive straitjacket" of Orientalism. I have pointed to anti-Orientalist texts by Milton Murayama, Louis Chu, Wayne Wang, and many Nisei writers, but I have made it very clear that they "belong to a different book," not one titled *The Deathly Embrace*. To chide me for failing to offer an alternative out of what I call the "Orientalist net" is like chiding Kafka for not restoring the beetle back to a human being. If some readers feel trapped by my book, I should say that it is far more desirable to face up to a potential malaise plaguing America, in particular Asian America, than to pretend that all is well. Ill tidings about one's self tend to be met with, at first, denial. Let the sharing of this book be a collective purge of neurosis in order to reach a new level of ethnic consciousness. After all, racial healing must begin with a remembrance of the nightmarish trauma. To ensure recovery, one ought to poke the scab to see if pus oozes out.

If I were to integrate "alternatives" — materials utterly incompatible with my subject — this might be a more agreeable book, especially to those readers who might personally identify with the topic. But the unique contribution this volume makes, as I see it, lies precisely in the un-relenting bearing down on "the deathly embrace." Perhaps only the fool-hardiness of an Asian immigrant inhabiting perpetual borderlands would lead me to cry out the truth about Asian Americans' new clothes. Being a naturalized alien, an Asian American by choice, I dangle between insider and outsider status, a double vision making it possible to exhibit their as well as my own nakedness — Orientalist stereotypes swathed in ethnic identity.

A second possible criticism is that this book contains personal refer-ences. Occasionally deviating from the traditional academic discourse of my first book, *Immigrant Subjectivities in Asian American and Asian Diaspora Literatures* (1998), I have integrated a handful of autobiograph-ical materials into this book, for I believe that scholarship has long sup-pressed the scholar's positionality, which is the root cause of scholarship. I wish to write not only from the head but also from the heart. However, I only use personal references — few and far between to begin with — when logical argumentation fails to deliver the message. Take, for in-stance, the end of chapter 2 on *Swiss Family Robinson*, where I refer to "Global Distribution [of Disney films] and Me," harking back to my first viewing of the film in my childhood in Taiwan and contrasting that with my then two-and-half-year-old daughter viewing the film with me in the United States. This autobiographical note is in fact the beginning of the chapter as well as the entire book. It is my hope that specialists reading this book have not been so co-opted that my appeal to memories and human warmth reads like an awkward aside.

Notes

Introduction

1. The rationale for choosing *Aiiieeeee!* as the title is echoed in the blurb on the back cover of the anthology: "*Aiiieeeee!* Until recently, that was the single sound assigned to one-dimensional Asian American caricatures in our movies, comic strips, and other mass media." To have *Aiiieeeee!* as the title is so pivotal to the editors' vision that they begin the introduction to *The Big Aiiieeeee!* (1991), the sequel to the 1974 anthology, with the identical explanation. In my *Immigrant Subjectivities in Asian American and Asian Diaspora Literatures* (1998), I commented that "[t]he choice of 'aiiieeeee!' as the title of the collection shows" "simultaneous disavowal and embracing of [Asian Americans'] otherness" and an attempt to "secure power from a cry of powerlessness. But this power relation buys into the essentialism of race based on the color of the skin ('white culture' versus 'yellow man'), the stereotype of the other as the perennial victim reduced to primal emotions, and, lastly, to the linguistic Orientalism of a scream (and perhaps a pain) unintelligible to the West. Among other things, this manifesto exposes the essentialism of the body and the linguistic reductionism the editors have implicitly accepted" (26).

1. Imagining the Orient in the Golden Age of Adventure Comics

For research on comic books, I am greatly indebted to the Special Collections at Michigan State University Library, especially the librarian Randall Scott.

1. The golden age of comic books is usually considered to be between the 1930s and the mid-1950s. Comic books constitute an area with different dynamics from newspaper comic strips and will not be included in this chapter.

2. Another version of events had Raymond quit the series in 1941 and Austin Briggs take over while using Raymond's signature.

3. Gina Marchetti, in *Romance and the "Yellow Peril": Race, Sex, and Discursive Strategies in Hollywood Fiction* (1993), views the "Yellow Peril" as intertwined with "medieval fears of Genghis Khan and Mongolian invasions of Europe" (2).

4. In a sequence in September 1941, months before the attack on Pearl Harbor, Alex Raymond portrayed a scene eerily similar to the imminent air war between the United States and Japan in the Pacific based on, I presume, the air war raging in the European theater.

2. Walt Disney's *Swiss Family Robinson*

1. In the revisionist spirit of the U.S. civil rights and global decolonization move ments, Jack Gold's film *Man Friday* (1976) starring Peter O'Toole and Richard Roundtree retells the story, in part, from Friday's point of view. In the scene where Crusoe asks Friday to race against him on the beach, Friday finds the idea of winning by beating one's opponents entirely absurd. The film thus questions the modern notion of competition. Another attempt at retelling through the eyes of the slave is Michel Tounier's *Friday* (1967).

2. Wyss's story gives an even more exaggerated treatment of the python episode. The python is stuffed and displayed in the family "museum."

3. It is intriguing to discover that many writers end their commentaries on adventure stories on a personal note, as I have chosen to do. Kenneth Maxwell, in his extensive review of the history of pirates, concluded with reminiscences of his childhood reading of *Treasure Island,* a present from his father. He also mentioned how pirates were adopted by "Disney World and dozens of Hollywood B movies" (37).

3. Martial Metaphors and Asian America

1. "Rafiki" probably derives from one of Dian Fossey's mountain gorillas by that name. Fossey publicized her study in Rwanda since the early 1970s in *National Geographic*. See Mariana Torgovnick's *Primitive Passions,* p. 95.

2. I asked Linda Lee Cadwell this question during a stop on her book promotion tour with John Little, who was entrusted with editing the Bruce Lee papers for the first three volumes of what was projected to be a twelve-volume set of "The Bruce Lee Library." The event took place on October 30, 1997, at the University Village Barnes and Noble Bookstore near the campus of the University of Washington, Seattle. Bruce and Linda Lee first met at the University of Washington.

3. Western film critics often compare Jackie Chan's performance to that of early cinema actors such as Buster Keaton.

4. Michelle Khan is Michelle Yeoh, who appears as the Bond girl with kung fu in *Tomorrow Never Dies* (1997).

5. This myth of the kung fu genre — triumphant despite the odds against the hero — seems particularly suited to Asians in the Western mind. The comparatively small stature of Asians in relation to Westerners already denotes disadvantage.

6. For detailed analysis of this passage in Kingston's *Tripmaster Monkey,* see chapter 2 of my *Immigrant Subjectivities in Asian American and Asian Diaspora Literatures* (1998).

7. I borrow from Fredric Jameson's distinction between pastiche and parody. For how the former eclipses the latter in postmodernism, see "Postmodernism and Consumer Society."

8. Just as the "mainstream" American reception of Kingston diverges strongly from some Asian American views, so does the Chinese reception depart from the American perspective. To illustrate just how wide the gap is between the Western and the Chinese receptions of Kingston and other Chinese American writers, let me draw from Hardy C. Wilcoxon's essay, "Chinese American Literature beyond the Horizon," based on the reaction of his Hong Kong students of Chinese descent at the University of Hong Kong. Wilcoxon finds that his students "intensely disliked *The Woman Warrior*, felt very uneasy with much of *M. Butterfly*, and felt alientated by 'exaggerations' and 'misconceptions' in even that most morally reassuring of books, *The Joy Luck Club* . . . a common theme unites nearly [all responses]: to a greater or lesser extent, these Asian American works tend to misrepresent and defame Chinese culture and Chinese people" (315–16). Not that the discontent felt by Hong Kong students should outweigh the praise from Western readers, but the different reactions stem from the antithetical positionalities of the two groups. Whereas Kingston's Orientalist style and strategies massage the self-image of the West, they directly threaten that of the East.

9. I wish to thank my then ten-year-old nephew Johnny Sun for introducing me to *Mortal Kombat*.

10. I concentrate on works with kung fu motifs that first appeared as video games. For instance, *The Karate Kid*, despite its box-office success and the many sequels, never appeared as a video game, so I did not include it in my discussion. Also, many novels for young adults, such as James Raven's *Dojo Rats: Test of Wills*, are likewise overlooked.

11. Christopher Lambert plays Lord Rayden in the film *Mortal Kombat* (1996). In one of the deeply Orientalist episodes, Asian monks at the so-called Temple of Light in China (but actually filmed in Thailand) kowtow to their God of Lightning, Lord Rayden, played by a Caucasian.

12. David Sheff reports in *Game Over* that "by 1990, one third of American homes would have one [Nintendo Entertainment System unit] — more than 30 million of them" (172). Yet this Nintendo dominance was overthrown by Sega in a few short years. "Sega has around 55 percent to 65 percent of the market," writes Kevin Maney in his 1995 *Megamedia Shakeout*. "Nintendo, 35 percent to 45 percent" (330).

4. Vincent Chin and Baseball

I wish to thank Douglas A. Noverr and Chi-Hsi Chao for their helpful comments on the drafts of this chapter. The views expressed here are, of course, my own.

1. I draw from three sources of legal documents on the Vincent Chin case: (1) *United States v. Ronald Ebens*, No. 83–60629-CR, Mich. Cir., Wayne Co. (March 16, 1983); (2) *United States v. Ronald Ebens*, 800 F.2d, pp. 1422–45 (1986); (3) *United States v. Ronald Ebens*, 654 F. Supp, pp. 144–46 (S.D. Ohio, 1987). Source 1 consists of three big boxes of unpublished court transcripts and documents; it has hundreds of volumes chronologically arranged from 1983 to 1987. It is housed in Chicago and can only be viewed through an arrangement with the U.S. District Court, Eastern District of Michigan in downtown Detroit. Source 2 is from *Federal Reporter*, and source 3 from *Federal Supplement*. To simplify in-text documentation, I will ab-

breviate references as "*US v. RE,*" followed by the case number and page number. Source 1 will also contain the volume number.

2. Girard's theory of the scapegoat perfectly explains the assault against Vincent Chin. To borrow from chapter 2, "Stereotypes of Persecution," in reviewing the Chin case, the first phase of "generalized loss of difference" in a crisis can be found in the layoffs and economic depression in the auto industry. The second step is what Girard calls "crimes eliminating differences," which occurred in the specific incident when Ebens made derogatory comments against all Asians indiscriminately. The third stage is the locating of victims marked by physical handicap or foreignness. The fourth stage is violence itself.

3. David Whitson finds that "sport has become one of the most important sites of masculinizing practices in cultures (and within classes) in which other kinds of physical prowess have become devalued and in which aggression is officially illegitimate" (28). Bruce Kidd makes a similar observation: "[R]ather than being an 'innocent' pastime, modern sports reinforce the sexual division of labor, thereby perpetuating the great inequality between the sexes and contributing to the exploitation and repression of both males and females" (250–51).

4. After having started to work on this project on Vincent Chin and baseball, I began to notice the disturbing merging of sports and sexploitation, Ebens's twin passions. Throughout the spring semester of 1996, I was repeatedly struck by an ad in the *State News*, Michigan State University's campus newspaper. This ad was put out by the local nude bar, Déjà Vu, displaying some sensuous women, around whom were arranged the captions: "FREE PASS. Wet Wednesday. Lansing's only all nude showbar. *Get in FREE with a Lugnuts ticket stub*" (my emphasis). The Lugnuts is the newly established Class A minor league baseball team in Lansing. Granted that the Lugnuts have no control over how Déjà Vu conducts its advertising, the coupling of sports and sexploitation is nevertheless only too clear.

5. Ebens and Nitz, two ordinary Americans who turned into murderers, remind one of ordinary Germans who became Nazis in World War II. Is a Nazi playing with his children at home after having supervised the gas chambers still a Nazi? Should we separate a Nazi at work and a Nazi at home? The defense clearly highlights Ebens the worker and the husband, whereas the prosecution focuses on Ebens the killer. The most disturbing question, however, is that it is one person, indivisible and whole.

6. Ametrius Vaughn, the barmaid and cashier at Fancy Pants, testified that Chin got single bills three times for the total amount of $150 in order to tip the dancers. Chin was clearly in a celebratory mood over his upcoming wedding nine days later, which turned into the day of his funeral.

7. See Elaine Kim, "Images of Asians in Anglo-American Literature," the opening chapter to her *Asian American Literature: An Introduction to the Writings and Their Social Context* (1982). Kim discovers that two archetypes dominate the image of Chinese males: Fu Manchu, created by Sax Rohmer; and Charlie Chan, developed by Earl Derr Biggers. Both stereotypes present effeminate Chinese males. See also the Prefaces to *Aiiieeeee!* and *The Big Aiiieeeee!* edited by Frank Chin et al.

8. The deliberately paradoxical final sentence evokes Joy Kogawa's description of the similar Japanese Canadian dilemma as they were treated by their fellow countrymen as "enemy aliens" during World War II. Kogawa's young protagonists in *Obasan* (1982) cast this in a riddle: "Stephen tells me. We are both the enemy and not the enemy" (70).

5. *The Chinese Siamese Cat*

1. Commenting on the character Jing-mei June Woo's embarrassment over her lower-class mother in *The Joy Luck Club,* Melani McAlister finds June "interpellated by the dominant Orientalist and middle-class discourse." But when the argument moves inevitably from June's alliance with bourgeois hegemony to the novelist's, McAlister hedges by simply observing that "Tan's silence . . . reverberates through the text" (115).

2. On the recommendation of his English tutor, the nearsighted, teenage emperor Pu Yi in Bernardo Bertolucci's *The Last Emperor* came into possession of a pair of spectacles.

3. The persistence of Orientalism is amazing when one consults the widely used *American Heritage Dictionary of the English Language* (3d edition) to look up "fan." The illustration to "fan" is a Western woman with the makeup of Madame Butterfly, whose waist and back are coquettishly curved. Her hand gesture is stylized and the right hand holds a collapsible fan.

4. *The Chinese Siamese Cat* is not paginated, so all references to the book contain no parenthetical documentation for page numbers.

6. "Chinese and Dogs" in *The Hundred Secret Senses*

1. Olivia feels that what she takes to be the cowherd can be, in San Francisco, "a doctoral student, a university lecturer, a depressed poet-activist" (293), hence highlighting the complexity of Asian and Asian American differences. What appears to be a native of the rural Changmian in China turns out to be a fellow Asian American.

2. The liquor or "local brew" introduced to the Bishops by the two Chinese women reminds one of the witches' brew in Shakespeare's *Macbeth.*

3. Both James Joyce in *Finnegans Wake* and Samuel Beckett in *Waiting for Godot* give variations of this word game.

7. Mulan Disney, It's Like, Re-Orients

1. The site in *Mulan* is the Hall of Supreme Harmony (*Taihedian*), which, as Jeffrey F. Meyer describes it in *The Dragons of Tiananmen* (1991), the Ming and Qing emperors used to preside over "the grand audiences, the most important being New Year, the winter solstice, and the emperor's birthday" (50).

2. The Disney portrayal of the nomadic tribes inhabiting northern China follows the implicitly derogatory description of them in *The Confucian Analects*: "*P'i-fa tso-jen*" ("Loosened hair and with coats buttoned on the left side").

8. Kazuo Ishiguro's Persistent Dream for Postethnicity

1. See Ishiguro's interview with Vorda and Herzinger, especially 133–34.

2. See Vorda and Herzinger, 135–36.

3. See Gregory Mason's "Inspiring Images" and his interview with Ishiguro, 336. See also Vorda and Herzinger, especially 147–48.

4. See Sheng-mei Ma, "Immigrant Schizophrenic in Asian Diaspora Literature," in *Immigrant Subjectivities in Asian American and Asian Diaspora Literatures* (1998), for a close analysis.

5. See Michael Rogin, *Blackface, White Noise: Jewish Immigrants in the Hollywood Melting Pot.*

6. The Merchant-Ivory film merges Mr. Lewis and Mr. Farraday into one. The senator played by Christopher Reeve not only attended the international conference at Darlington Hall but purchased it years later, hence highlighting the passing of an old era. The man who criticized Darlington at the conference became the owner of Darlington Hall.

7. This ascent in an elevator resembles Alice's fall through the rabbit-hole in Lewis Carroll's *Alice's Adventures in Wonderland.* Both the ascent and the descent occur in slow motion that freezes time and warps space, thereby justifying the surrealist episodes to follow.

8. The concluding sentence is a rephrasing of the last sentence of *An Artist of the Floating World.*

Bibliography and Filmography

Althusser, Louis. "Ideology and the Ideological State Apparatuses (Notes Towards an Investigation)." In *Lenin and Philosophy and Other Essays*, trans. Ben Brewster. New York: Monthly Review Press, 1971. 127–86.

Anderson, Benedict. *Imagined Communities: Reflections on the Origin and Spread of Nationalism*. London: Verso, 1983.

Andriola, Alfred. *Charlie Chan*. Papeete, Tahiti: Comics Stars in the World, 1976.

Arendt, Hannah. *Eichmann in Jerusalem*. 1963. New York: Viking, 1966.

Bacho, Peter. "The Second Room." In *Dark Blue Suit and Other Stories*. Seattle: University of Washington Press, 1997. 39–53.

Bakhtin, M. M. *The Dialogic Imagination*. Ed. Michael Holquist, trans. Caryl Emerson and Michael Holquist. Austin: University of Texas Press, 1981.

———. *Rabelais and His World*. Trans. Helene Iswolsky. Cambridge: MIT Press, 1968.

Barshay, Robert. "Ethnic Stereotypes in *Flash Gordon*." Unpublished paper presented at the Popular Culture Association; a copy of the paper housed at the Special Collections of the Michigan State University Library, 1973.

Bataille, Georges. *Eroticism*. New York: Walker and Company, 1962.

Baudrillard, Jean. *Simulacra and Simulation*. Trans. Sheila Faria Glaser. Ann Arbor: University of Michigan Press, 1994.

Bhabha, Homi K., ed. *Nation and Narration*. New York: Routledge, 1990.

Biggers, Earl Derr. *The House without a Key*. 1925. New York: Triangle, 1940.

Blanchard, Kendall. *The Anthropology of Sport: An Introduction*. Westport, Conn.: Bergin and Garvey, 1995.

Block, Alex Ben. *The Legend of Bruce Lee*. New York: Dell, 1974.

Bloom, Harold. "Introduction." In *Robinson Crusoe: Major Literary Characters*, ed. Harold Bloom. New York: Chelsea House, 1995. 1–3.

Blythe, Will. "Remains of the Night." Review of *The Unconsoled*, by Kazuo Ishiguro. *New York*, October 16, 1995, 64–65.

Brody, Jennifer DeVere. "Hyphen-Nations." In *Cruising the Performative: Interventions into the Representation of Ethnicity, Nationality, and Sexuality*, ed. Sue-Ellen Case, Philip Brett, and Susan Leigh Foster. Bloomington: Indiana University Press, 1995. 149–62.

Browne, Nick. "The Undoing of the *Other* Woman: Madame Butterfly in the Discourse of American Orientalism." In *The Birth of Whiteness: Race and the Emergence of U.S. Cinema*, ed. Daniel Bernardi. New Brunswick, N.J.: Rutgers University Press, 1996. 227–56.

Buck, Elizabeth B. "Asia and the Global Film Industry." *East-West Film Journal* 6.2 (July 1992): 116–33.

Bulosan, Carlos. *America is in the Heart.* 1946. Seattle: University of Washington Press, 1973.

Butler, Judith. *Gender Trouble: Feminism and the Subversion of Identity.* New York: Routledge, 1990.

Caniff, Milton. *Damma Exile: Four Complete Steve Canyon Adventures.* (Materials originally run in 1956 and 1957.) Princeton, Wis.: Kitchen Sink Press, 1991.

———. *Male Call: 1942–1946.* Ed. Peter Poplaski. Princeton, Wis.: Kitchen Sink Press, 1987.

———. *Terry and the Pirates.* Color Sundays from 1934 to 1946. 12 vols. New York: Flying Buttress, 1990–93.

———. *Terry and the Pirates: China Journey.* New York: Nostalgia Press, 1977.

"The Case for Vincent Chin: A Tragedy in American Justice." The Official Statement of American Citizens for Justice. Royal Oak, Michigan, May 11, 1983.

Chan, Sucheng. *Asian Americans: An Interpretive History.* Boston: Twayne Publishers, 1991.

Cheung, King-Kok. *Articulate Silences: Hisaye Yamamoto, Maxine Hong Kingston, Joy Kogawa.* Ithaca, N.Y.: Cornell University Press, 1993.

———, ed. *An Interethnic Companion to Asian American Literature.* New York: Cambridge University Press, 1997.

Cheung, King-Kok, and Stan Yogi. *Asian American Literature: An Annotated Bibliography.* New York: Modern Language Association, 1988.

Chiao, Hsiung-ping. "Bruce Lee: His Influence on the Evolution of the Kung Fu Genre." *Journal of Popular Film and Television* 9.1 (spring 1981): 30–42.

Chin, Frank. *The Chickencoop Chinaman and The Year of the Dragon: Two Plays.* Seattle: University of Washington Press, 1981.

Chin, Frank, Jeffrey Paul Chan, Lawson Fusao Inada, and Shawn Wong, eds. *Aiiieeeee!: An Anthology of Asian American Writers.* 1974. New York: Mentor, 1991.

———, eds. *The Big Aiiieeeee!: An Anthology of Chinese American and Japanese American Literature.* New York: Meridian, 1991.

The Chinese Connection. Directed by Lo Wei. With Bruce Lee. Golden Harvest, 1972.

Chu, Louis. *Eat a Bowl of Tea.* 1961. New York: Lyle Stuart, 1990.

Constable, Nicole. *Christian Souls and Chinese Spirits: A Hakka Community in Hong Kong.* Berkeley: University of California Press, 1994.

Defoe, Daniel. *Robinson Crusoe.* 1719. New York: Oxford University Press, 1972.

Deutscher, Isaac. "The Non-Jewish Jews." *The Non-Jewish Jews and Other Essays.* London: Oxford University Press, 1968.

Dickstein, Morris. "After Utopia: The 1960s Today." In *Sights on the Sixties*, ed. Barbara L. Tischler. New Brunswick, N.J.: Rutgers University Press, 1992. 13–23.

Dixon, Robert. *Writing the Colonial Adventure: Race, Gender and Nation in Anglo-Australian Popular Fiction, 1875–1914.* New York: Cambridge University Press, 1995.

Enter the Dragon. Directed by Robert Clouse. With Bruce Lee. Warner Brothers, 1973.

Espiritu, Yen Le. *Asian American Panethnicity: Bridging Institutions and Identities.* Philadelphia: Temple University Press, 1992.

Fenn, William Purviance. *Ah Sin and His Brethren in American Literature.* (Delivered before the Convocation of the College of Chinese Studies, June 1933.) Peiping, China: College of Chinese Studies cooperating with California College in China, 1933.

Fists of Fury. Directed by Lo Wei. With Bruce Lee. Golden Harvest, 1971.

Fong, Timothy P. *The First Suburban Chinatown: The Remaking of Monterey Park, California.* Philadelphia: Temple University Press, 1994.

Frazee, Steve. *Swiss Family Robinson.* Illustrated by Henry Luhrs. Authorized edition adapted from the Walt Disney motion picture *Swiss Family Robinson.* Racine, Wis.: Whitman, 1960.

"FREE PASS. Wet Wednesday. Lansing's only all nude showbar. Get in FREE with a Lugnuts ticket stub." *State News,* April 10, 1996, p. 14, and April 17, 1996, p. 14.

Freud, Sigmund. "Creative Writers and Day-Dreaming." In *The Freud Reader,* ed. Peter Gay. New York: W. W. Norton, 1989. 436–43.

Game of Death. Directed by Robert Clouse. Golden Harvest, 1977.

Garber, Marjorie. *Vested Interests: Cross-dressing and Cultural Anxiety.* New York: Routledge, 1992.

Giles, Jeff. "Shoot the Piano Man; Ishiguro Gets Bloated." Review of *The Unconsoled,* by Kazuo Ishiguro. *Newsweek,* October 2, 1995, 92F.

Girard, Rene. *Scapegoat.* Trans. Yvonne Freccero. Baltimore: Johns Hopkins University Press, 1986.

Giroux, Henry A. *Fugitive Cultures: Race, Violence, and Youth.* New York: Routledge, 1996.

Goellnicht, Donald C. "Tang Ao in America: Male Subject Positions in *China Men.*" In *Reading the Literatures of Asian America,* ed. Shirley Geok-lin Lim and Amy Ling. Philadelphia: Temple University Press, 1992. 191–212.

Gomery, Douglas. "Disney's Business History: A Reinterpretation." In *Disney Discourse: Producing the Magic Kingdom,* ed. Eric Smoodin. New York: Routledge, 1994. 71–86.

Gramsci, Antonio. *Prison Notebooks.* New York: Columbia University Press, 1992.

Green, Martin. *Dreams of Adventure, Deeds of Empire.* New York: Basic Books, 1979.

Hagedorn, Jessica. *Charlie Chan Is Dead: An Anthology of Contemporary Asian American Fiction.* New York; Penguin, 1993.

Hanegraaff, Wouter J. *New Age Religion and Western Culture: Esotericism in the Mirror of Secular Thought.* New York: E. J. Brill, 1996.

Harvey, Robert C. *The Art of the Funnies: An Aesthetic History.* Jackson: University of Mississippi Press, 1994.

Hirabayashi, Lane, ed. *Teaching Asian America: Diversity and the Problem of Community.* Boulder, Colo.: Rowman and Littlefield, 1997.

Hom, Marlon K. Review of *Eat a Bowl of Tea. Amerasia Journal* 6.2 (1979): 95–98.

———, ed. *Songs of Gold Mountain: Cantonese Rhymes from San Francisco Chinatown.* Berkeley: University of California Press, 1987.

Hongo, Garrett. *Under Western Eyes: Personal Essays from Asian America.* New York: Anchor, 1995.

Honour, Hugh. *Chinoiserie: The Vision of Cathay.* New York: Dutton, 1962.

Horkheimer, Max, and Theodor W. Adorno. *Dialectic of Enlightenment.* Trans. John Cummins. New York: Herder and Herder, 1944.

Hwang, David Henry. *The Dance and the Railroad.* In *FOB and Other Plays.* New York: Plume, 1990. 51–86.

———. *M. Butterfly.* New York: Penguin, 1986.

Ishiguro, Kazuo. *An Artist of the Floating World.* 1986. New York: Vintage, 1989.

———. *A Pale View of Hills.* 1982. New York: Vintage, 1990.

———. *The Remains of the Day.* 1989. New York: Knopf, 1990.

———. *The Unconsoled.* New York: Knopf, 1995.

Ishiguro, Kazuo, and Oe Kenzaburo. "The Novelist in Today's World: A Conversation." In *Japan in the World,* ed. Masao Miyoshi and H. D. Harootunian. Durham, N.C.: Duke University Press, 1993. 163–76.

Jacobson, Dawn. *Chinoiserie.* London: Phaidon, 1993.

Jameson, Fredric. "Postmodernism and Consumer Society." In *Postmodernism and Its Discontents: Theories, Practices,* ed. E. Ann Kaplan. New York: Verso. 1988. 13–29.

Jen, Gish. *Mona in the Promised Land.* New York: Plume, 1996.

———. *Typical American.* New York: Plume, 1992.

———. *Who's Irish?* New York: Knopf, 1999.

Jung, C. G. *Pychology and Religion: West and East.* Trans. R. F. C. Hull. New York: Pantheon, 1958.

Kadohara, Cynthia. *The Floating World.* New York: Ballantine, 1989.

———. *In the Heart of the Valley of Love.* New York: Penguin, 1992.

Kaminsky, Stuart M. *American Film Genres.* 2d. ed. Chicago: Nelson-Hall, 1985.

———. "Kung Fu Film as Ghetto Myth." In *Movies as Artifacts: Cultural Criticism of Popular Films,* ed. Michael T. Marsden, John G. Nachbar, and Sam L. Grogg Jr. Chicago: Nelson-Hall, 1982. 137–45.

Kent, Stephen A. "Slogan Chanters to Mantra Chanters: A Deviance Analysis of Youth Religious Conversion in the Early 1970s." In *Sights on the Sixties,* ed. Barbara L. Tischler. New Brunswick, N.J.: Rutgers University Press, 1992. 121–33.

Kidd, Bruce. "Sports and Masculinity." In *Beyond Patriarchy: Essays by Men on Pleasure, Power, and Change,* ed. Michael Kaufman. New York: Oxford University Press, 1987. 250–65.

Kim, Elaine H. *Asian American Literature: An Introduction to the Writings and Their Social Context.* Philadelphia: Temple University Press, 1982.

———. "Defining Asian American Realities through Literature." In *The Nature and Context of Minority Discourse,* ed. Abdul R. JanMohamed and David Lloyd. New York: Oxford University Press, 1990. 146–70.

———. Foreword. *Reading the Literatures of Asian America.* Ed. Shirley Geok-lin Lim and Amy Ling. Philadelphia: Temple University Press, 1992. xi–xvii.

Kimberly, Marion. *Swiss Family Robinson.* Comic Book. New York: Gallery, 1991.

Kimmel, Michael S. "Baseball and the Reconstruction of American Masculinity, 1880–1920." In *Sport, Men, and the Gender Order: Critical Feminist Perspectives,* ed. Michael A. Messner and Donald F. Sabo. Champaign, Ill.: Human Kinetics Books, 1990. 55–65.

Kingston, Maxine Hong. *China Men.* New York: Knopf, 1980.

———. "Cultural Mis-readings by American Reviewers." In *Asian and Western Writers in Dialogue: New Cultural Identities,* ed. Guy Amirthanayagam. London: Macmillan, 1982. 55–65.

———. *Hawaii One Summer.* Woodcuts by Deng Ming-Dao. San Francisco: Meadow, 1987.

———. *Tripmaster Monkey: His Fake Book.* New York: Knopf, 1989.

———. *The Woman Warrior: Memoirs of a Girlhood among Ghosts.* New York: Knopf, 1976.

Kirihara, Donald. "The Accepted Idea Displaced: Stereotype and Sessue Hayakawa." In *The Birth of Whiteness: Race and the Emergence of U.S. Cinema,* ed. Daniel Bernardi. New Brunswick, N.J.: Rutgers University Press, 1996. 81–99.

Kogawa, Joy. *Itsuka.* 1992. New York: Anchor, 1994.

———. *Obasan.* Boston: David R. Godine, 1982.

Lai, Him Mark, Genny Lim, and Judy Yung. *Island: Poetry and History of Chinese Immigrants on Angel Island, 1910–1940.* Seattle: University of Washington Press, 1991.

Lake, Carlton. *In Quest of Dali.* New York: Putnam, 1969.

Lee, Robert G. *Orientals.* Philadelphia: Temple University Press, 1999.

Lewis, Jon. *The Road to Romance and Ruin: Teen Films and Youth Culture.* New York: Routledge, 1992.

Lim, Shirley Geok-lin. "Asians in Anglo-American Feminism: Reciprocity and Resistance." In *Changing Subjects: The Making of Feminist Literary Criticism,* ed. Gayle Greene and Coppelia Kahn. New York: Routledge, 1993. 240–52.

———. "Assaying the Gold: Or, Contesting the Ground of Asian American Literature." *New Literary History* 24 (1993): 147–69.

———. *Writing South East Asia in English: Against the Grain, Focus on Asian English-Language Literature.* London: Skoob Books, 1994.

Lin Yutang. *My Country and My People.* 1935. New York: John Day, 1939.

Ling, Amy. *Between Worlds: Women Writers of Chinese Ancestry in the U.S.* New York: Pergamon, 1990.

Lipsitz, George. "The Possessive Investment in Whiteness: Racialized Social Democracy and the 'White' Problem in American Studies." *American Quarterly* 47.3 (September 1995): 369–87.

Liu Wu-chi. *An Introduction to Chinese Literature.* Bloomington: Indiana University Press, 1966.

Liu Wu-chi and Irving Yucheng Lo, eds. *Sunflower Splendor: Three Thousand Years of Chinese Poetry.* Bloomington: Indiana University Press, 1975.

Ma, Sheng-mei. *Immigrant Subjectivities in Asian American and Asian Diaspora Literatures.* Albany: State University of New York Press, 1998.

Man Friday. Directed by Jack Gold. With Peter O'Toole and Richard Roundtree. Incorporated Television Company, 1976.

Maney, Kevin. *Megamedia Shakeout: The Inside Story of the Leaders and the Losers in the Exploding Communications Industry.* New York: John Wiley and Sons, 1995.

Marchetti, Gina. *Romance and the "Yellow Peril": Race, Sex, and Discursive Strategies in Hollywood Fiction.* Berkeley: University of California Press, 1993.

Mason, Gregory. "An Interview with Kazuo Ishiguro." *Contemporary Literature* 30.3 (fall 1989): 335–47.

———. "Inspiring Images: The Influence of the Japanese Cinema on the Writings of Kazuo Ishiguro." *East-West Film Journal* 3.2 (June 1989): 39–52.

Maxwell, Kenneth. "Pirate Democracy." Review of *Under the Black Flag: The Romance and the Reality of Life among the Pirates,* by David Cordingly. *New York Review of Books* 44.4 (March 6, 1997): 34–37.

McAlister, Melani. "(Mis)reading *The Joy Luck Club.*" *Asian American: Journal of the Culture and the Arts* 1 (winter 1992): 102–18.

Menand, Louis. Review of *The Unconsoled,* by Kazuo Ishiguro. *New York Times Book Review,* October 15, 1995, 7.

Meyer, Jeffrey F. *The Dragons of Tiananmen: Beijing as a Sacred City.* Columbia: University of South Carolina Press, 1991.

Milton, Joyce. *The Yellow Kids: Foreign Correspondents in the Heyday of Yellow Journalism.* New York: Harper and Row, 1989.

Mintz, Marilyn D. *The Martial Arts Films* South Brunswick. A. S. Barnes, 1978.

Miyoshi, Masao. *Off Center: Power and Culture Relations between Japan and the United States.* Cambridge: Harvard University Press, 1991.

Mori, Toshio. *Yokohama, California.* 1949. Seattle: University of Washington Press, 1985.

Moy, James. "The Death of Asia on the American Field of Representation." In *Reading the Literatures of Asian America,* ed. Shirley Geok-lin Lim and Amy Ling. Philadelphia: Temple University Press, 1992. 349–57.

Mukherjee, Bharati. *Jasmine.* New York: Fawcett Crest, 1989.

———. *Wife.* New York: Fawcett Crest, 1975.

Murayama, Milton. *All I Asking for Is My Body.* 1959. Honolulu: University of Hawaii Press, 1988.

Noverr, Douglas A. and Lawrence E. Ziewacz. "Violence in American Sports." In *Sports in Modern America,* ed. William J. Baker and John M. Carroll. Saint Louis: River City Publishers, 1981. 129–45.

Outcault, Robert Fenton. *The Yellow Kid: A Centennial Celebration of the Kid Who Started the Comics.* Northampton, Mass.: Kitchen Sink Press, 1995.

Owen, Rob. *Gen X TV: The Brady Bunch to Melrose Place.* Syracuse, N.Y.: Syracuse University Press, 1997.

Palumbo-Liu, David, ed. *The Ethnic Canon: Histories, Institutions, and Interventions.* Minneapolis: University of Minnesota Press, 1995.

Paper Angels. Written by Genny Lim, Directed by John Lone. American Playhouse. PBS. 1985.

Polan, Dana. "Brief Encounters: Mass Culture and the Evacuation of Sense." In *Studies in Entertainment: Critical Approaches to Mass Culture,* ed. Tania Modleski. Bloomington: Indiana University Press, 1986. 167–87.

Prebish, Charles. "*Karma* and Rebirth in the Land of the Earth-Eaters." In *Karma and Rebirth: Post Classical Developments,* ed. Ronald W. Neufeldt. Albany: State University of New York Press, 1986. 325–38.

Raven, James. *Dojo Rats: Test of Wills.* New York: Bantam, 1993.

Raymond, Alex Gillespie. *Flash Gordon.* 5 Vols. (Materials originally run from 1934 to 1943.) Princeton, Wis.: Kitchen Sink Press, 1990–92.

———. *Flash Gordon: Escapes to Arboria.* Vol 3. (Materials originally run from October 31, 1937, to March 5, 1939.) New York: Nostalgia Press, 1977.

———. *Flash Gordon: Into the Water World of Mongo.* Vol 2. New York: Nostalgia Press, 1974.

———. *Flash Gordon Joins the Power Men.* Vol 5. (Materials originally run from April 14, 1940, to July 6, 1941.) New York: Nostalgia Press, 1978.

———. *Flash Gordon: The Planet Mongo.* Vol 1. New York: Nostalgia Press, 1974.

———. *Flash Gordon Versus Frozen Horrors*. Vol 4. (Materials originally run from March 12, 1939, to April 7, 1940.) New York: Nostalgia Press, 1978.

Render, Sylvia Lyons, ed. *The Short Fiction of Charles W. Chestnutt*. Washington, D.C.: Howard University Press, 1974.

Return of the Dragon. Directed by Bruce Lee. With Bruce Lee. Golden Harvest and Concorde, 1972.

Rogin, Michael. *Blackface, White Noise: Jewish Immigrants in the Hollywood Melting Pot*. Berkeley: University of California Press, 1996.

Rohmer, Sax. *The Mystery of Dr. Fu Manchu* (originally published as *The Insidious Dr. Fu-Manchu*). 1913. London: J. M. Dent and Sons, 1985.

Rorem, Ned. Review of *The Unconsoled*, by Kazuo Ishiguro. *Yale Review* 84.2 (April 1996): 154–59.

Rothfork, John. "Zen Comedy in Postcolonial Literature: Kazuo Ishiguro's *The Remains of the Day*." *Mosaic* 29/1 (March 1996): 79–102.

Rushing, Janice Hocker, and Thomas S. Frentz. *Projecting the Shadow: The Cyborg Hero in American Film*. Chicago: University of Chicago Press, 1995.

Said, Edward. *Culture and Imperialism*. New York: Knopf, 1993.

———. *Orientalism*. New York: Pantheon, 1978.

Sartre, Jean-Paul. *Anti-Semite and Jew*. Trans. George J. Becker. New York: Schocken Books, 1948.

Schroeder, Randy. "Playspace Invaders: Huizinga, Baudrillard and Video Game Violence." *Journal of Popular Culture* 30.3 (winter 1996): 143–53.

Sheff, David. *Game Over: How Nintendo Zapped an American Industry, Captured Your Dollars, and Enslaved Your Children*. New York: Random House, 1993.

Shen, Gloria. "Born of a Stranger: Mother-Daughter Relationships and Storytelling in Amy Tan's *The Joy Luck Club*." In *International Women's Writing: New Landscapes of Identity*, ed. Anne E. Brown and Marjanne E. Gooze. Westport, Conn.: Greenwood, 1995. 233–44.

Shih, Vincent Y. C. *The Taiping Ideology: Its Sources, Interpretations, and Influences*. Seattle: University of Washington Press, 1967.

Smoodin, Eric, ed. *Disney Discourse: Producing the Magic Kingdom*. New York: Routledge, 1994.

Spacks, Patricia Meyer. *The Adolescent Idea: Myths of Youth and the Adult Imagination*. New York: Basic Books, 1981.

Steinberg, Sybil. Review of *The Unconsoled*, by Kazuo Ishiguro. *Publishers Weekly*, September 18, 1995, 105–6.

Sue, Stanley, and James K. Morishima. *The Mental Health of Asian Americans*. San Francisco: Jossey-Bass Publishers, 1982.

Sui Sin Far. *Mrs. Spring Fragrance and Other Writings*. Ed. Amy Ling and Annette White-Parks. Urbana and Chicago: University of Illinois Press, 1995.

Swiss Family Robinson. Directed by Ken Annakin. With John Mills, Dorothy McGuire, James MacArthur, Janet Munro, and Sessue Hayakawa. Walt Disney, 1960.

Tan, Amy. *The Chinese Siamese Cat*. Illustrated by Gretchen Schields. New York: Macmillan, 1994.

———. *The Hundred Secret Senses*. New York: Putnam, 1995.

———. *The Joy Luck Club*. New York: Putnam, 1989.

———. *The Kitchen God's Wife*. New York: Putnam, 1991.

————. *The Moon Lady.* Illustrated by Gretchen Schields. New York: Macmillan, 1992.

Torgovnick, Marianna. *Gone Primitive: Savage Intellects, Modern Lives.* Chicago: University of Chicago Press, 1990.

————. *Primitive Passions.* New York: Knopf, 1997.

Tounier, Michel. *Friday.* 1967. Trans. Norman Denny. Baltimore: Johns Hopkins University Press, 1997.

Uelmen, Amelia J. *Seeing the U.S.A.: The Landscapes of Walt Disney.* Washington, D.C.: Georgetown University Press, 1991.

United States v. Ronald Ebens, No. 83–60629-CR, Mich. Cir., Wayne Co. (March 16, 1983).

United States v. Ronald Ebens. 800 F.2d, pp. 1422–45 (1986).

United States v. Ronald Ebens. 654 F. Supp, pp. 144–46 (S.D. Ohio, 1987).

Van Ash, Cay, and Elizabeth Sax Rohmer. *Master of Villainy: A Biography of Sax Rohmer.* London: Tom Stacey, 1972.

Verne, Jules. *The Castaways of the Flag: The Final Adventures of the Swiss Family Robinson.* New York: Grosset and Dunlap, 1924.

————. *Their Island Home: The Later Adventures of the Swiss Family Robinson.* New York: Grosset and Dunlap, 1924.

Vorda, Allan, and Kim Herzinger. "An Interview with Kazuo Ishiguro." *Mississippi Review* 20.1/2 (1991): 131–54.

Wagner, Rudolf G. *Reenacting the Heavenly Vision: The Role of Religion in the Taiping Rebellion.* Berkeley: University of Berkeley China Research Monograph 25. 1982.

Waley, Arthur. *Chinese Poems.* 1946. London: George Allen and Unwin, 1962.

————, trans. *Monkey (Hsi-yu chi).* By Wu Cheng-en. New York: Grove, 1943.

Wall, Kathleen. "*The Remains of the Day* and Its Challenges to the Theories of Unreliable Narration." *Journal of Narrative Technique* 24.1 (winter 1994): 18–42.

Weller, Robert P. *Resistance, Chaos and Control in China: Taiping Rebels, Taiwanese Ghosts and Tiananmen.* Seattle: University of Washington Press, 1994.

Whitson, David. "Sport in the Social Construction of Masculinity." In *Sport, Men, and the Gender Order: Critical Feminist Perspectives,* ed. Michael A. Messner and Donald F. Sabo. Champaign, Ill.: Human Kinetics Books, 1990. 19–30.

"Who Killed Vincent Chin?" Directed by Christine Choy and Renee Tajima. PBS. 1988.

Wilcoxon, Hardy C. "Chinese American Literature beyond the Horizon." *New Literary History* 27 (1996): 313–28.

Wilhelmus, Tom. "Between Cultures." Review of *The Unconsoled,* by Kazuo Ishiguro. *Hudson Review* 49.2 (summer 1996): 321–22.

Winchester, Mark D. "Holy Gee, It's a War!!! The Yellow Kid and the Coining of 'Yellow Journalism.' " *Inks: Cartoon and Comic Art Studies* 2.3 (November 1995): 22–37.

Wong, Jade Snow. *Fifth Chinese Daughter.* 1945. Seattle: University of Washington Press, 1989.

Wong, Sau-ling Cynthia. "Denationalization Reconsidered: Asian American Cultural Criticism at a Theoretical Crossroads." *Amerasia Journal* (Double issue on the theme "Thinking Theory in Asian American Studies") 21.1/2 (1995): 1–27.

————. "Ethnicizing Gender: An Exploration of Sexuality as Sign in Chinese Immigrant Literature." In *Reading the Literatures of Asian America,* ed. Shirley Geok-lin Lim and Amy Ling. Philadelphia: Temple University Press, 1992. 111–29.

———. *Reading Asian American Literature: From Necessity to Extravagance.* Princeton, N.J.: Princeton University Press, 1993.

———. "'Sugar Sisterhood': Situating the Amy Tan Phenomenon." In *The Ethnic Canon: Histories, Institutions, Interventions.* Ed. David Palumbo-Liu. Minneapolis: University of Minnesota Press, 1995. 174–210.

———. "Teaching Chinese Immigrant Literature: Some Principles of Syllabus Design." In *Reflections of Shattered Windows: Promises and Prospects for Asian American Studies,* ed. Gary Y. Okihiro, Shirley Hume, Arthur A. Hansen, and John M. Liu. Pullman: Washington State University Press, 1988. 126–34.

Wood, Michael. Review of *The Unconsoled,* by Kazuo Ishiguro. *New York Review of Books,* December 21, 1995, 17–18.

Wu, William F. *The Yellow Peril: Chinese Americans in American B Fiction, 1850-1940.* Hamden, Conn.: Archon, 1982.

Wyndham, Francis. "Nightmare Hotel: Kazuo Ishiguro Battles the Mores of an Imaginary Country." Review of *The Unconsoled,* by Kazuo Ishiguro. *New Yorker,* October 23, 1995, 90–94.

Wyss, Johann David. *The Swiss Family Robinson.* Translated from the original German. Ed. William H. G. Kingston with ninety-five illustrations on wood. London and New York: George Routledge and Sons, 18–.

Yamamoto, Hisaye. *Seventeen Syllables and Other Stories.* Lathem, N.Y.: Kitchen Table (Women of Color Press), 1988.

Index

Sheng-mei Ma is associate professor in the Department of American Thought and Language at Michigan State University, specializing in Asian American studies and Holocaust/genocide studies. He is the author of *Immigrant Subjectivities in Asian American and Asian Diaspora Literatures.*